REEDS

VHF-D

HANDBO

C000104584

Other titles of interest

GMDSS: A User's Handbook 2edn by Denise Bréhaut
ISBN 0 7136 6224 7

Anyone with GMDSS equipment on board their vessel will need an operator's licence. This book explains the operation of the system as a whole and the procedures involved, as well as covering the syllabi of the General Operator's Certificate (GOC), the Restricted Operator's Certificate (ROC), the Long Range Certificate (LRC) and the Short Range Certificate (SRC).

Communications at Sea by Mike Harris
ISBN 0 7136 6271 9

A complete guide to all forms of communication at sea. It examines the international marine use of mobile phones, satellites, amateur radio and email, cutting through the sales hype to enable readers to make the right choice for their needs and sailing territory. An essential on board reference for cruising sailors worldwide.

Understanding Weatherfax 2edn by Mike Harris
ISBN 0 7136 6122 4

A concise guide to the procedures and techniques for receiving weatherfax charts and satellite images, via radio, satellite or the internet. The book also explains how to interpret the information from these charts and images into meaningful weather forecasts, and interpret the early warning signs of a storm.

The Adlard Coles Book of Electronic Navigation by Tim Bartlett
ISBN 0 7136 5715 4

Using plain English to strip away the jargon, this book sets out to demystify the technology behind modern marine electronics and to explain how the various systems work and how to get the best out of the equipment available. Aimed at anyone with an interest in navigating small craft, but particularly those working towards their Day Skipper, Yachtmaster and other RYA courses.

To order a copy visit www.adlardcoles.com or call MDL on 01256 302692

REEDS

VHF-DSC
HANDBOOK

Second edition

S<small>UE</small> F<small>LETCHER</small>

ADLARD COLES NAUTICAL
LONDON

ACKNOWLEDGEMENTS

I would like to thank the following people for their help and encouragement in the writing of this book. My grateful thanks go to:

Kim Fisher, head of Navigation and Communication for the Maritime Coastguard Agency, for his valuable advice and endless patience.

Rod Fletcher, who heroically read the manuscript several times for technical accuracy and who sorted out my word processor when it mutinied.

Alison Noice, RYA National SRC Advisor for her advice.

HM Coastguard for their advice and use of material.

Published by Adlard Coles Nautical
an imprint of A & C Black Publishers Ltd
38 Soho Square, London W1D 3HB
www.adlardcoles.com

Copyright © Sue Fletcher 2006

First edition published by Thomas Reed Publications 1997
Second edition published by Adlard Coles Nautical 2006

ISBN-10: 0-7136-7573-X
ISBN-13: 978-0-7136-7573-3

All rights reserved. No part of this publication may be reproduced in any form or by any means – graphic, electronic or mechanical, including photocopying, recording, taping or information storage and retrieval systems – without the prior permission in writing of the publishers.

The author, Sue Fletcher, has asserted his/her right under the Copyright, Designs and Patents Act, 1988, to be identified as the author of this work.

A CIP catalogue record for this book is available from the British Library.

A & C Black uses paper produced with elemental chlorine-free pulp, harvested from managed sustainable forests.

Typeset in 10.5 on 12 pt Rotis Serif.
Printed and bound in Singapore by Tien Wah Press Pte Ltd.

Note: While all reasonable care has been taken in the production of this publication, the publisher takes no responsibility for the use of the methods or products described in the book.

CONTENTS

FOREWORD

by Kim Fisher

When this book was first published, GMDSS was a worrying threat to the leisure sailor; heralding an unwelcome change from an established radio-communication system to the unknown. Now, eight years later, GMDSS is an established system that has demonstrated its use and value.

The Global Maritime and Safety System (GMDSS) is the latest development in marine communications, following on from the original Morse system of the 1980s, through the radiotelephone systems of the 1920s, the VHF system of the 1950s and satellite systems of the 1970s. It introduces an element of automation to marine communications that has the advantage of reducing workload on a vessel by obviating the need for a continual listening watch on calling channels. It is also a shore-based system, the emphasis being on enabling a vessel to always signal to the shore. In this way, a vessel is never beyond radio range of someone who can offer assistance. The world's merchant fleet all converted to GMDSS by 1999 and have been relying on the system ever since.

The voluntary radio user, who does not have to carry radio under international conventions, has found great benefit in the past in adopting the systems developed for the merchant ship and sharing in the available safety and information services. Adopting GMDSS techniques gives the voluntary user an opportunity to take advantage of the infrastructure put in around the world for GMDSS and of maintaining compatibility with merchant shipping.

Small craft sailors, who typically stay within VHF range of the shore, have long experience of carrying VHF radio. The GMDSS adds a new feature to the VHF radio with the introduction of Digital Selective Calling (DSC). This permits other vessels to be called up by their identity number and also provides a button that will generate a distress alert which contains the position of the vessel. These features all reduce the load on the traditional calling channel 16 and obviate the need for listening continually on the channel. Many Coastguards have fitted DSC equipment in their coast stations and can react to a distress alert and provide assistance. Merchant ships can also be called even if they are not listening on channel 16

This book sets out to describe the leisure craft VHF-DSC radio system in detail and shows how it is used in the Global Maritime Distress and Safety System. With a little training as described, the average sailor will have no difficulty in mastering VHF-DSC and can move forward into the world of GMDSS.

Kim Fisher
Head of Navigation and
Communication
UK Maritime and Coastguard Agency

INTRODUCTION

How it all started

One wonders if Marconi knew the genie he was releasing when he discovered radio. It is not an exaggeration to say that it has revolutionised all our lives as communication, entertainment and education are available at the press of a button.

In 1896 Marconi brought his newly developed wireless from Italy to London. At that time we were the number one sea power and fully understood the benefit of good ship communication. The first ship fitted was the *East Goodwin Lightship*, which had a link to South Foreland Lighthouse. This was an inspired choice because, in 1899, the *SS RP Matthews* ran the lightship down and the lifeboat was summoned by radio. In 1912, through the use of radio, the whole world soon knew the fate of the *Titanic* and although a few lives were saved, many died. Ships near to the *Titanic* did not operate a radio watchkeeping regime and so did not receive her Distress messages. The technology of the day also limited radio working to Morse code. This involved radio officers listening for the SOS message which had only just been internationally standardised.

Since those early pioneering days, radio has evolved in much the same way as our road system, even down to describing radio messages as radio 'traffic'. In the beginning there was Morse code, akin to one man and his cart making his way up a single, muddied track. He got there, but it was slow. Today we demand high-speed, high-volume communications, which has meant adopting digital technology so that messages get there fast – just like traffic on a motorway.

Digital technology has revolutionised almost every aspect of our lives yet it has been accepted and absorbed to the point that we wonder how we ever did without it. The latest evolution of VHF radio, Digital Selective Calling also utilises digital technology and is the reason for this book.

ABOUT THIS BOOK

The book is divided into two parts – Radio Theory (Chapters 1–9) and Radio Practice, (Chapters 10–19). Each has a quiz at the end to help you see how much you've learned. I've tried to arrange this book so that you can approach it from a variety of angles depending on your need:

- If you're taking the Short Range Certificate or the DSC update module, there is everything you need to know, including 70 quiz questions with answers to check your understanding.

- If you're just brushing up on the new system, a glance down the contents tables will lead you straight to your chosen subject.

- If you already know your way around VHF radio but want to be steered button by button around the DSC Controller, just select the type of call you want to make from the colour coded contents tables.

- If you are looking for tips on how to get more from your radio, they are marked with a lighthouse and tinted for quick reference.

- If you need to look up the procedure for a particular call there is the Quick Call Guide.

My main aim in writing this book is to introduce you to VHF-DSC radio in as straightforward and non-technical a way as possible. Just as there is no need to know the intricate workings of the internal combustion engine in order to drive a car, you don't need to know the finer points of radiowave propagation to speak into a microphone.

• PART 1 •
RADIO THEORY

1· Global Maritime Distress and Safety System

Before the use of radio, a ship sailed over the horizon and was then out of communication until it reappeared over someone else's horizon at its destination. Some ships never reappeared and their fate remains forever unknown. The introduction and evolution of radio on board ships significantly reduced the number of losses but it has not completely eliminated them and it is a sad fact that around ten ships a year still sail into the wide blue yonder and are never seen again. The bulk carrier *The Derbyshire* and the fishing vessel *Gaul* are just two memorable examples.

Something needed to be done and this task was taken on by the International Maritime Organisation (IMO) based in London. The first stage was to set up INMARSAT – a satellite service for ships. This ensured that ships always had a communication link with the shore from anywhere in the world and did not have to rely on having another ship within radio range. Then the IMO developed its Global Maritime Distress and Safety System (GMDSS) and in February 1992 began phasing it in gradually.

The basic concept of the GMDSS is that search and rescue organisations ashore, as well as shipping in the vicinity of the vessel or person in distress, will be rapidly alerted to a distress incident so that they can assist in a co-ordinated search and rescue operation with the minimum of delay. The system also provides for Urgency and Safety communications and the broadcast of navigational and meteorological warnings.

Compulsory compliance with the GMDSS only applies to cargo ships over 300 tons and most vessels that carry more than 12 passengers. In GMDSS jargon these are known as 'Convention Ships'. All other vessels are classed as 'Voluntary Fit'. This includes leisure craft.

The basic requirement of GMDSS requires that all Convention Ships must be able to send and receive a distress call to a Rescue Co-ordination Centre by at least two independent means. To do this they must carry:

- An Emergency Position Indicating Radio Beacon (EPIRB) that transmits a Distress signal over the INMARSAT system or the COSPAS/SARSAT distress satellite system.

3

● Radios that use a more sophisticated calling facility provided by Digital Selective Calling (DSC) and this in turn allows all radio watchkeeping to be automatic.

With automatic watchkeeping there is no longer a mandatory requirement for a ship's radio operator to listen on CH16. They may choose to do so if practicable, but this cannot be relied upon. In 2005, however, most ships were still listening

It is not compulsory to fit a VHF-DSC radio. If you have an older, non-DSC equipped VHF radio and do not wish to change to GMDSS you can continue to use your radio to talk to other vessels. The Coastguard no longer operate a dedicated CH16 watch using headphones but operate the watch using a loudspeaker.

GMDSS and its benefits are there for you if you are prepared to install the Digital Selective Calling equipment.

GMDSS AREAS

Under the GMDSS the radio equipment that merchant ships must carry depends on the sea areas in which they trade. To this end, the world has been divided into four areas:

Area A1 within range of shore-based VHF coast stations fitted with DSC (20-30) miles.

Area A2 within range of shore-based MF coast stations fitted with DSC (100 miles).

Area A3 within the coverage area of INMARSAT satellites (between 70°N and 70°S).

Area A4 the remaining sea areas using HF DSC.

This book is for the vessels that operate in the A1 area.

GMDSS

Below is a list of the equipment that is included in the GMDSS, most of which will only be carried by commercial vessels. Strict regulations apply to the type of equipment carried by shipping, but because this book is for the leisure sailor there is no need to explain the carriage requirements of a liner. With this in mind the following table offers a more realistic breakdown of the type of boating undertaken by leisure craft and makes equipment recommendations based on those criteria.

RECOMMENDED EQUIPMENT

	Area of Operation from coast (Nautical Miles)				
	Up to 5M	Up to 30M	Up to 60M	Up to 150M	Worldwide
Handheld waterproof VHF radio – also for use in a liferaft	✔	✔	✔	✔	✔
VHF-DSC fixed radio installation	✔	✔	✔	✔	✔
406MHz EPIRB with 121.5MHz for homing and GPS for position	O	O	O	✔	✔
MF-DSC SSB radio	✘	✘	O	✔	✔
INMARSAT	✘	✘	O	O	✔
Navtex receiver	O	O	✔	✔	✔
Search and Rescue Radar Transponder (SART)	✘	O	O	✔	✔
HF-DSC SSB radio	✘	✘	✘	✘	✔

Key: ✔ – Recommended; O – Optional; ✘ – Not Required

In many parts of Europe you are requested to call the local Coastguard using DSC and you will eventually need DSC to call ships. So now is the time to consider joining the new system.

The UK and most of the mainland European coast stations are now fitted for VHF CH70 Digital Selective Calling (DSC). This means that there will be increasingly less watchkeeping on traditional calling channels, although the UK Coastguard has stated that it will maintain a watch on CH16 for 'the foreseeable future'. However, there may come a time when this service could be withdrawn.

When you buy your new DSC equipment, you will need to apply for a 9-digit Maritime Mobile Service Identity (MMSI) number and program it into the set. This acts like a telephone number and with it you can call Coastguard stations and other vessels. In the event of distress, a dedicated button allows you to make a DSC Distress Alert that automatically sends your MMSI number and position provided that the DSC is interfaced with a GPS receiver. Any Coastguard station or DSC-equipped vessel within your radio range will hear it. Once the call has been acknowledged communication is continued by voice on CH16.

DSC is simply a digital front-end to normal voice communication that calls and activates an alarm on the selected DSC radio. This allows automatic watchkeeping and is as much a step forward on marine radio as direct dialling was on the terrestrial telephone service.

2 • RED TAPE

THE REGULATING AUTHORITIES

The regulations governing the use of maritime radio are set by the International Telecommunication Union (ITU) and the Wireless Telegraphy Act 1949. The management of radio communications in the UK is the responsibility of Ofcom. Licence administration is handled by the Radio Licensing Centre on behalf of Ofcom.

It is an offence to install or use any radio equipment on board a UK vessel without obtaining a radio licence first. Ofcom employs a team of inspectors whose job it is to check that all vessels with a radio have a licence. If a vessel has a radio but no licence, the owner is likely to face a heavy fine and confiscation of the equipment.

THE SHIP RADIO LICENCE

Like the Vehicle Licence, the Ship Radio Licence is renewable annually. New VHF installations are not inspected as a matter of routine but random spot checks are made periodically by radio inspectors. They have powers to immediately confiscate unlicensed equipment and prosecute the owner. The Ship Radio Licence and your Operator's Certificate must be kept on board for inspection by an authorised officer of any government.

> **Foreign administrations may confiscate the radio equipment where a valid licence cannot be produced on demand.**

The Ship Radio Licence will allow you to install and use any of the following maritime radio equipment:

- MF (Medium Frequency), HF (High Frequency), VHF (Very High Frequency) and UHF (Ultra High Frequency) Radio.
- Satellite communications equipment.
- Radar.

7

- Hand-held VHF or UHF radios.
- Emergency Position Indicating Radio Beacons (EPIRBs).
- SART.

This licence only covers the radio installation, not the operator, and the annual cost (at the time of writing) is £20. In return you will receive a licence disc that looks almost identical to your car licence disc and which must be displayed on the port-hand side of the vessel to enable any inspector to see that your radio installation is legal. You also receive a Licence Terms booklet and a Licence Document. The document gives identification details and the vessel's 'Public Correspondence Category' – HX. This means that you do not have to maintain a daily radio watch. Other licence holders have the category H24, where they have to keep a radio watch 24 hours a day.

If you sell your vessel, you must send details of the new owner to the Radio Licensing Centre. If you have purchased a vessel you will need to make a new application to obtain a licence, as a Ship Radio Licence does not transfer when the ownership of the vessel changes.

If you need to apply for a Ship Radio Licence contact the Radio Licensing Centre (contact details under Useful Addresses).

Future reforms

At the time of writing, there are proposals to reform licensing rules to reduce the regulatory burden. Ofcom plans to set up an online, web-based, self-service, free-of-charge licensing system thereby removing the yearly renewal process and fee. This new approach offers users an easier way to comply with legal obligations and use radio equipment that is appropiately licensed. Ofcom is proposing to:

- Remove the need for radio owners to purchase a new licence each year. Instead, a ship radio licence would be valid for the life of the vessel.
- Provide a web-based licensing service as an alternative to the postal service.
- Issue electronic licences free of charge to users of the web-based service.
- Continue to offer a postal service for applicants that do not have access to, or prefer not to use the internet based system. This service would incur a fee, which at this time has not yet been determined.

The onus to have a radio licence remains and the licencee will be required to keep all details up to date eg a change in vessel ownership. This will be available in the free online service, with the option of choosing a postal service that would incur a small administrative charge.

This deregulation will still require a vessel's radio to have a valid licence and it will still continue to be an offence not to have a ship radio licence both in UK waters and abroad. Failure to carry a valid licence will still carry penalties of a fine and confiscation of the radio equipment.

A licence is required even if the equipment is not in constant use or if it is only used for distress purposes – so get legal now.

RED TAPE

SHIP PORTABLE RADIO LICENCE

A Ship Portable Radio Licence covers the use of a portable, handheld marine VHF or VHF-DSC radio with an integral power supply and antenna which is not already covered by a Ship Radio Licence for a fixed radio. It can also additionally cover the carrying of a 406MHz or 121.5MHz personal locator beacon (PLB). This licence is usually issued to someone who intends using a handheld radio on more than one vessel. It is issued with a 'T' reference as opposed to a vessel callsign and it is usual to use the vessel name as the identifier because of this.

CERTIFICATE OF COMPETENCE

Just as every driver needs a licence to drive a car, operators of marine radios also require a licence. This licence is designed to maintain operating standards; provide knowledge of distress, urgency and safety procedures; and instruct the user about the regulations that apply to marine communications. The services provided through the marine VHF radio are professional services, so operators must be professional in their use. The only way that this can be achieved is for every operator to be trained.

The training for the Short Range Certificate is managed by the Royal Yachting Association (RYA). It is a relatively short course, typically one day, that culminates with a multi-choice question paper and a simple practical assessment carried out by an approved assessor. Once you have passed the test you will be granted a licence. This licence is just like the car driver's licence in that it is held for life and it has two parts:

- Part one is the Certificate of Competence that indicates you have been trained to use the equipment.
- Part two is your Authority to Operate. If you break the radio regulations, your authority to operate can be withdrawn.

It is permitted for anyone to use the VHF radio provided that any untrained operator is closely supervised by someone with an Authority to Operate.

If you already hold an existing VHF Certificate of Competence you will have to attend a short update course in the use of Digital Selective Calling before you fit VHF-DSC to your vessel. **The Authorities do not permit DSC to be used by untrained operators.**

A VHF-DSC operator's certificate is also an integral part of the RYA Cruising scheme. It is a mandatory requirement for both RYA Coastal Skipper and Yachtmaster® Offshore certificates of competence and is a desirable qualification for students studying for the RYA Day Skipper certificate.

If you have difficulty finding a course in your area, or want more information, contact the RYA. Details are available under Useful Addresses at the end of the book.

SPECIFIC REQUIREMENTS FOR RADIO EQUIPMENT

Under the Radio Equipment and Telecommunications Terminal Equipment Regulations 2000, which implements the EU Directive 99/5/EC (the RE&TTE Directive), it is a legal requirement that all radio equipment meets certain essential requirements. It is the responsibility of any person who places radio equipment on the market to ensure that the requirements of the RE&TTE Directive are met and that the equipment is marked with the CE marking. Information must also be supplied to the user on the intended use of the equipment.

In 2000 the RE&TTE Directive replaced the old 'type approval' regime. Any equipment approved before that date under the older 'type approval' regime can still continue to be used.

This legislation is designed to ensure that all marine radios:

- Avoid interference to others.
- Perform in a hostile environment.
- Work correctly in accordance with international agreements for the safety of life at sea.

If you have any doubts about the specification of a particular piece of radio equipment contact Ofcom for advice.

RED TAPE

You are strongly advised to check that the equipment you intend to purchase is fully approved otherwise no licence can be granted and any radio inspector could confiscate it. Generally speaking, reputable suppliers only sell approved equipment. However, with the growth in boat jumbles and internet auction sites, you may be very tempted to buy foreign or ex-military equipment, neither of which is likely to be approved for UK vessels. Cheap sets made for the US market will not have the correct channels for European use.

THE CALLSIGN

A callsign will be allocated to your vessel when the radio equipment on the vessel is first licensed. The callsign is rather like the registration number of a car and stays with the vessel for life even if there is a change of ownership or vessel name. The callsign is recognised worldwide because Ofcom registers it with the ITU along with the details you give about your vessel. Each month, and each year when you re-licence the vessel, the details are updated with the ITU. Because the callsign identifies a vessel when you travel internationally, you must inform Ofcom of any changes to the vessel name or ownership.

A callsign is unique and generally consist of four letters and one number. As well as providing a unique identification, the first digit (or two) indicates the stations nationality. The first digit of all British Radio stations is G or Z or 2.

A portable, hand-held VHF radio used on one vessel alone is classed as a fixed radio but if it is used on more than one vessel it is classed

as a transportable radio. Owners of this type of radio will be issued
with a 'T' reference number. The 'T' sign attached to the transportable
radio is unique so each individual radio must be licensed separately.
You will not be able to make telephone calls through foreign coast
radio stations.

MARITIME MOBILE SERVICE IDENTITY

A Maritime Mobile Service Identity (MMSI) is a unique 9-digit number
and is the equivalent of an electronic callsign. It acts in the same way
as a telephone number.

Ship stations: the first three digits indicate nationality and the last six
identify the individual station. For example:

                232   123456
                 ↑   ↑
          National Code   Individual Station Identity

Coast stations: the first two digits are 00 followed by the country
code, followed by the individual station number. For example:

         00   232   0014
          ↑   ↑   ↑
   Shore station code   Country code   Individual station
                                               number

The MMSI allows you to make automatic calls through your Digital
Selective Calling equipment and is the identity your equipment transmits when you are in distress. An MMSI number for portable
equipment has coding within the numbers to indicate that the radio is
likely to be used on more than one vessel.

To obtain an MMSI number for your vessel you must apply to
Ofcom. You will be assigned your 9-digit number, which is then programmed into your new DSC equipment either by your supplier, by the
owner of the radio. If your radio is owner-programmable be careful to
note the instructions as some equipment only permits a certain number

of attempts. The DSC operation of your equipment is inhibited until the vessel's MMSI number has been programmed into it.

The MMSI number, like the callsign, stays with the vessel. If you sell the vessel but take the VHF radio for use on your next vessel, you will have to apply for a new MMSI number and have the new number entered by a radio engineer.

MMSI numbers of Coastguards are listed in almanacs and the Admiralty List of Radio Signals.

Note National Codes for the UK are 232, 233, 234 and 235.

THE RADIOTELEPHONE LOG

Commercial vessels are required to keep a radio telephone log – a diary of radio calls. Pleasure craft are not required by law to keep a log, but it is prudent to keep a reasonable record of significant radio working, eg if you discuss collision avoidance with another vessel. It is essential to keep a record of Distress and Urgency working. These details can be kept in the ship's log rather than in a separate book.

DOCUMENTS TO BE CARRIED

Vessels voluntarily fitted with VHF Radiotelephones must carry the following documents:

- The Ship Radio Licence.
- The certificate(s) of the operator(s).
- A list of the coast stations with whom you are likely to communicate. These are contained in *Reeds Nautical Almanac* and *The Admiralty List of Radio Signals Volume 1 (ALRS Vol. 1)*. There is now an *ALRS Small Craft (NP 289)*.
- A ship's logbook or radiotelephone logbook.

For quick reference, keep a note of your vessel's callsign and MMSI number displayed close to the radio and in your logbook.

3 • THE DIGITAL SELECTIVE CALLING RADIO

WHAT IS A DSC RADIO?

Functionally, a DSC radio could be regarded as a cross between a telephone and a traditional Marine VHF radio all rolled into one unit. The Digital Selective Calling function, known as the DSC Controller, simply sends a burst of digital code that will 'ring' another DSC radiotelephone by triggering an alarm. Once the call has been accepted, the equivalent of lifting a normal phone's receiver, you use the radio in the usual way. No doubt Sod's Law will be in force, ensuring that it 'rings' at just the wrong moment, so if the call remains unanswered, the details will be stored in the Received Calls Log.

There are several classes of DSC Controller, each with differing capabilities for different applications.

- The **Class A** Controller is fitted to ships that operate in all sea areas more than 300 miles offshore. These fully comply with GMDSS requirements.
- The **Class B** Controller is fitted to ships that operate up to 300 miles from the coast. These comply with the minimum GMDSS requirements.
- The **Class D** Controller is a 'budget' controller, fitted to voluntary fit vessels and intended to provide minimum VHF-DSC facilities that may not fully comply with the minimum requirements of the GMDSS. For example it will not be possible to acknowledge a DSC Distress call using DSC on a Class D Controller. Most leisure craft will fit this type.

THE FIXED RADIO CONTROLS AND FUNCTIONS

The illustration (opposite) of the controls of a typical DSC radio' and the explanation below of the functions found on a typical VHF-DSC radio are very general indeed. Each manufacturer will base the radio

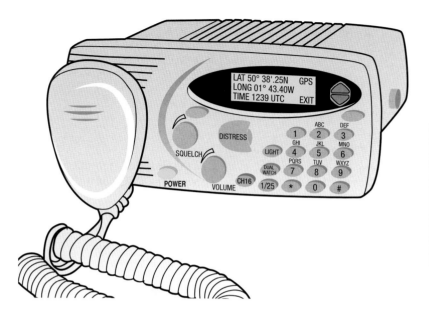

The controls of a typical VHF-DSC radio

on the laid-down specification but each will produce a unique radio. Some radios will have many additional features, whilst others will be very basic. In a book of this type it would be impossible to give details of all the radios available, or indeed second-guess what features may be included in the future. The short history of the mobile phone is a good illustration of the speed at which electronics develop. This book is no substitute for the handbook that comes with your chosen radio.

The most common features are as follows.

Display screen: Ideally, this needs to be large and clear, but the physical size of the radio is likely to limit the screen size. Its function is to:

- Show the menu items under consideration.
- Prompt the operator if an incorrect operation is attempted.
- Display error messages.
- Display incoming and logged calls.
- Display the current position derived from the NMEA interface with the vessel's GPS (if fitted). When using the DSC Controller for Urgency, Safety and Routine calling, position is **not** included in the call.

Position is only included in Distress calls. The radio should be able to take direct position input from the vessel's GPS through the normal NMEA connection. This option is to be preferred, as the position will be continually updated. In the event of failure, for any reason, an error message will show and the position and time will have to be loaded manually through the numeric keypad and 'Enter' or 'OK' button.

- Display the time.
- Indicate that a message is being transmitted (TX) or received (RX).
- Display the power level selected.

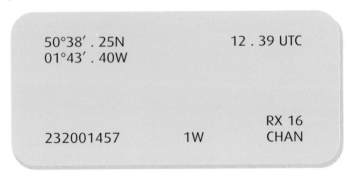

The display screen in radio mode

Power switch: This is usually an independent switch or is often incorporated into the volume control knob. A light will indicate that the set is turned on.

Menu button: This switches on the DSC Controller. When the DSC Controller has been inactive for five minutes the radio will automatically revert to the radio mode and display the above screen.

Cancel/clear button: Check with your instruction book as the use of this button varies from set to set.

Enter: Used to enter/confirm/send a selected menu item.

Scroll ▲▼ buttons: These allow you to scroll up or down through the menu available. When you find the item you want simply press ENTER.

Distress button: This clearly identified button allows DSC Distress calls to be transmitted. To prevent accidental operation it is covered with a spring-loaded cover. You will see and hear that a Distress call has been initiated but there is a five-second time delay between initially pressing the button and the call being sent. This is to prevent false alarms. Operation differs between sets so check the instructions.

Numeric keypad: For entering channel numbers, MMSIs, and manual position information. Most radios are also fitted with alphabet keys for use with any text-based functions.

Channel 16 dedicated button: This is the primary channel for passing Distress messages by voice and until all stations convert to using DSC for calling, it will remain the general calling channel. On pressing the CH16 dedicated button the radio will automatically switch to high power.

Hi/Lo power switch: The maximum power output for a UK yacht is 25 watts and is used for all Distress and Urgency working and calls to the Coastguard. Low power is one watt and where possible this should be selected in all other circumstances to avoid undue interference to other stations.

Squelch control: Radio is subject to a lot of background noise that you hear as a hiss, which overpowers the signal you want to hear. The squelch control filters out this hiss, but if you turn the knob too far you will filter out the signal as well. Turn it just enough to cut out the noise but no more.

Microphone: incorporating the **Press To Transmit (PTT) switch** and on many current sets a channel and 1/25 watt selection as well. When you press the PTT switch, your radio becomes a transmitter and you speak. When you release the switch, the radio reverts to being a receiver and you listen. The PTT switch cannot be locked on but when the microphone is not in use, store it where the PTT switch cannot be accidentally pressed. If it is accidentally activated you will relay to everyone around the sounds of life aboard your vessel. It is not unknown for a vessel to have its domestic radio tuned to Radio 1 and the ship's radio tuned to CH16. With the PTT switch activated it rebroadcasts Radio 1 on CH16, jamming the channel for up to a 30-mile radius.

Transmitting indicator: Red LED or TX on the display.

THE DSC RADIO

Dual watch facility: This allows the operator to monitor CH16 and one other channel at the same time without having to switch manually between channels. Transmitting is not possible when dual watch is switched on. On some sets dual watch is automatically switched off when the handset is lifted from its hook, or when the PTT switch is pressed. When this happens the radio will generally tune to the optional channel, not CH16. If you want CH16 to be selected, push the dedicated CH16 button. Icom and Simrad say that their sets will monitor CH70. One receiver is used exclusively for CH70 and the other toggles between the channels.

 Fit a hook or cradle to store the microphone when it is not in use.

Scan and Memory: The button labels could be any of the following: PSCN, PSC, MS, SCN, R/D, TAG, CALL, MEM, M+, M-, CLR. This facility allows you to monitor and program into the radio's memory any number of channels you wish. The scanner sequentially moves from one channel to the next in turn, stopping where a signal is detected. Once again, CH70 cannot be included in this mode.

DIM or a light symbol: Background illumination for keys and/or display.

SITING THE RADIO

The set should be fastened firmly in a convenient position that allows you to use and read the controls easily. It must be sited away from heat, the steering compass, the engine, sea spray and dampness. When fitting the radio the installation manual should give you the minimum safe distance it can be fitted from the steering compass.

The radio must be sited clear of weather so it is usual for it to be in the cabin of a small boat. To make it easier to use, a waterproof speaker sited close to the steering position, but not next to the steering compass, is a definite asset. It allows the person on watch to monitor the radio without disturbing crew sleeping below. An extension transmitter microphone handset may also be useful.

PORTABLE RADIO

For small or relatively open boats a handheld set is almost the only option when it comes to choosing a radio. A portable is also used as a back-up to a fixed set and, because it is a completely self-contained unit, it will work when the main electrical supply fails or the vessel has been dismasted.

Confusingly, there are portable sets sold as GMDSS Transportable, that are intended for use in survival craft on merchant ships when it is desirable to have a portable radio to communicate with the rescue craft during the final stages of a rescue. They are generally coloured a bright orange or yellow and DO NOT have a DSC capability. They have a limited number of channels and require special non-rechargeable batteries.

In the future, when portable VHF-DSC sets are readily available on the market, it is hoped that they will come with an integral GPS in order that position can be included in any Distress Alert. Currently a portable radio must be connected to an external GPS in just the same way that any fixed set is, but when the unit is used away from that connection, eg in a liferaft, the position becomes increasingly misleading. After 23.5 hours the position will be erased to prevent false position/time information being transmitted.

Disadvantages

Compared with a fixed set, any handheld suffers three disadvantages:

1 Limited battery capacity
2 Low antenna height
3 Low transmitting power

To take each disadvantage in turn:

Limited battery capacity: Transmitting consumes battery power rapidly. Advances in battery technology help extend the time but transmitting will always be restricted.

Talk time can be significantly increased by:

- Using low power (one watt) whenever possible. It is good for at least two miles.
- Planning what you're going to say before pressing the button.

THE DSC RADIO

- Keeping calls brief.
- Ensuring that you're understood the first time by speaking clearly in plain English.
- Choosing equipment that can accept regular alkaline batteries. These are readily available and can be kept on board, fully charged, until required.
- Wherever possible, not wasting time calling other vessels on CH16 but calling direct on an agreed working channel.

Low antenna height: The VHF radio signal is limited by the VHF horizon, which is approximately five miles when talking to another boat also using a handheld. (More on this later in the book.) If you have a masthead antenna you can double this.

Low transmitting power: High power in a handheld is 5 watts compared to 25 watts on a fixed set. This is to preserve battery power. It is possible to increase the effective transmitting output of the radio by up to 40 per cent by using a high-gain masthead antenna. The problems encountered with these antennas are that they are about 2m (6ft 7in) long and only work well when upright. If you have a small boat that spends most of its time heeled this option is not for you.

None of the problems is insurmountable, but if your boat allows for it then opt for a fixed radio as the primary radio. You'll get more facilities, more transmitting power, more talk time and a greater signal range. However, it is a good idea to have at least one portable radio on board as it will offer these advantages:

- It can be used in the vessel's tender for communications with the primary vessel.
- It can be used in a distress situation to speak to rescuers.
- In a larger vessel it can be used for communications between the helm and the foredeck.

4 · EPIRBs

WHAT IS AN EPIRB?

An Emergency Position Indicating Radio Beacon – EPIRB – is a self-contained battery operated radio transmitter, which is both watertight and buoyant. It is the closest thing we have to a 'Beam me up Scottie' device. Its purpose is to transmit a Distress Alert and then to mark the position of survivors in a Search and Rescue operation and should be carried as a supplement to a marine radio, not an alternative. If sailing more than a few miles off the coast, it makes sense to have an alternative means of calling for help. Once activated, an EPIRB should not be switched off until the rescue has been completed. As soon as it is over it is important that the EPIRB is deactivated.

Types of EPIRB

Only one type of EPIRB is approved for use in the UK. This uses 406.025MHz with the addition of 121.5MHz for homing-in purposes. A COSPAS/SARSAT satellite will pick up the 406MHz Distress signal and pass it down to the Rescue Co-ordination Centre (RCC). The RCC will re-transmit the Distress Alert to ships in the vicinity of the vessel in distress and instigate other Search and Rescue procedures. The 406MHz EPIRB has a unique identification code which identifies the vessel on which it is carried, and it is a *legal* requirement to register it. Registration contact details are available in the Useful Addresses section of the book.

The latest generation of EPIRBs has GPS capability, giving the precise location of survivors. When a 406MHz EPIRB is activated, the Rescue Co-ordination Centre will contact the registration database who will be able to supply information on the size and type of craft in distress. If you purchase a second-hand satellite EPIRB, make sure you re-register it with the relevant database otherwise the rescue services will be looking for the wrong boat! The location accuracy is approximately three miles.

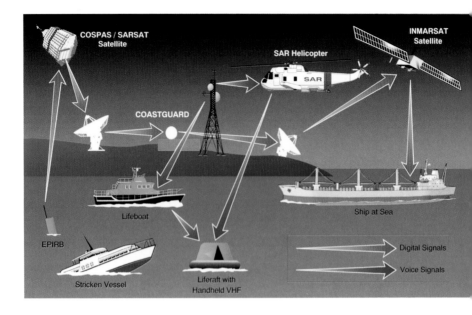

The EPIRB Distress Alert System

Older 121.5MHz only devices are no longer recommended for use as EPIRBs. This signal cannot be stored by satellite and any monitoring will be phased out ib the near future. However, they are recommended for homing purposes in search and rescue situations.

LOCATION AND CARE OF THE EPIRB

The EPIRB should be stowed where it can be ready for use but it must not be tied to the vessel as an EPIRB that goes down with the vessel will not work. You can fit a hydrostatic release mechanism that allows the EPIRB to float free but if you do this, check the hydrostatic release regularly and replace it in line with the manufacturer's recommendation. An EPIRB that is allowed to just float free is more likely to mark the position of the wreck so ensure that you collect it and attach it to the liferaft. Ensure that other pieces of gear, especially anything with magnetic properties, cannot accidentally activate it or its magnetic relay. To prevent false alarms, mount it somewhere dry if it has a salt-water activated battery.

An EPIRB that is taken off the vessel for any reason should be deactivated in line with the manufacturer's instructions. On occasion EPIRBs have been tracked doing 80mph in the back of their owner's cars and every year the authorities waste a great deal of time and money tracing EPIRB false alarms. It must be remembered that false alarms mask genuine distresses in the same area. If you accidentally activate your EPIRB, tell the Coastguard immediately. Do not turn it off until told to do so by the Coastguard.

If you take your EPIRB home for safekeeping, wrap it in several layers of aluminium foil. This provides radio frequency screening if it is accidentally activated.

EPIRBs

5 · SEARCH AND RESCUE TRANSPONDER (SART)

The SART is a radar transponder that operates on 9GHz when activated by a vessel using a (3cm) wavelength radar. Its purpose is to assist a Search and Rescue aircraft or vessel to locate survivors during a Search and Rescue operation.

When a searching vessel activates a SART, 12 distinctive dots will appear on its radar screen. As the searching vessel gets closer to the SART, the dots form arcs and finally, when in close proximity, the arcs form concentric circles.

SART shows 12 dots | Dots change to arcs as Search and Rescue vessel gets closer | In close proximity the radar screen shows concentric circles

The picture of a SART on a radar screen

A SART has a battery life of 96 hours in standby mode and 8 hours when it is transmitting but it only transmits whilst a radar signal is interrogating it. From a liferaft to a searching ship the transmitting range is approximately five miles but increases to 30 miles for a searching aircraft. The signal range to a ship can be increased by extending the pole to its maximum and by mounting the SART as high as possible.

The SART should be routinely checked for signs of damage and the battery must be replaced at the end of its life.

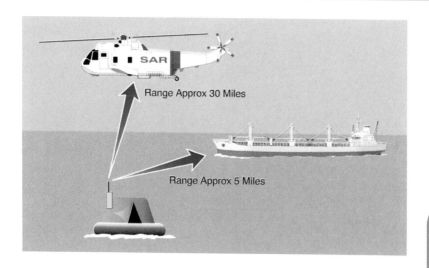

Range of a Search and Rescue Transponder

SART

WARNING: Only use a SART when you are in distress, and on no account consider using a SART to replace a radar reflector, or radar target enhancer. Its signal is an internationally recognised distress signal and any false alert could render you liable for prosecution.

Do not use a SART and a radar reflector together as the radar reflector could prevent the SAR's radar from seeing the SART.

6 • NAVTEX

Navtex is a worldwide information system that provides a print-out of essential navigation and weather information in English. It can be thought of as NAVigation TEXt. It has been developed to provide a low cost, simple means of receiving marine safety information on board vessels in coastal waters. It is an integral part of the GMDSS that provides information to help vessels navigate safely.

It is transmitted on two frequencies, 518kHz and 490kHz. 518kHz is for use worldwide whilst 490kHz has been introduced for use in the language of a country to provide local information, primarily for small craft. This information supplements the coastal waters English language 518kHz Navtex service.

In the UK, the availability of 490kHz has given the opportunity to provide dedicated forecasts for waters up to 12 miles offshore. Regular transmissions covering the UK coastal waters are now made from three transmitters twice per day and include a very useful three-day outlook.

To gain full benefit from the service, dedicated equipment is recommended. The special equipment comprises a small unit containing a receiver, fixed-tuned to the Navtex frequencies, and uses either a screen or a continuous paper feed for displaying the messages received. The receiver is left switched on continuously and may be programmed to automatically receive only selected stations and/or categories of messages. For example, if you do not have Loran-C on board there is no need for you to receive messages relating to Loran-C, so you can de-select these. This saves paper and time. Certain categories of message on some sets cannot be deselected by the receiver, ie, navigational and meteorological warnings and search and rescue information.

A micro-processor control ensures that a routine message already received will not be reprinted on subsequent transmissions and also that messages will not be printed unless the received signal is strong enough to ensure good copy.

Interference between stations is avoided by time-sharing the frequency and limiting the range of transmitters to around 300 miles. Each station has a ten-minute transmitting 'slot' every four hours and details can be found in *Reeds Nautical Almanac* and in the *Admiralty*

List of Radio Signals (ALRS) Volume 3. Three stations cover the UK: Niton, Cullercoats and Portpatrick.

The world is divided into NAVAREAs and the UK is in NAVAREA 1. Each Navtex station has an identification letter that you program into your receiver. This ensures that you only receive information that applies to the area for which the broadcast station is responsible. By studying your planned route you can program into your receiver the stations that will be most relevant to you.

The stations closest to the UK in Navarea 1 are listed with their station identity letter on the table below:

518kHz Navtex Stations in NAVAREA I:

Country	Station Name	Station ID	Range (nm)
BELGIUM	OOSTENDE (THAMES)	M	150
BELGIUM	OOSTENDE	T	50
FRANCE	CORSEN	A	300
IRELAND	MALIN HEAD	Q	400
IRELAND	VALENTIA (DUBLIN)	W	400
NETHERLANDS	DEN HELDER	P	250
NORWAY	ROGALAND	L	450
UNITED KINGDOM	PORTPATRICK	O	270
UNITED KINGDOM	CULLERCOATS	G	270
UNITED KINGDOM	NITON	E	270
UNITED KINGDOM	NITON (N. FRANCE)	K	270

490kHz Navtex Stations in NAVAREA I:

Country	Station Name	Station ID	Range (nm)
UNITED KINGDOM	PORTPATRICK	C	270
UNITED KINGDOM	NITON (N. FRANCE)	T	270
UNITED KINGDOM	NITON	I	270
UNITED KINGDOM	CULLERCOATS	U	270

A four-character group prefixes each message. The first character is the code letter of the transmitting station, eg Niton = E, the second character indicates the category of the message (see table) and the third and fourth are message serial numbers. 00 denotes urgent traffic such as gale warnings and are always printed.

MESSAGE CATEGORIES

A Navigational warnings

B Meteorological warnings

C Ice reports

D Search and Rescue information

E Weather forecasts

F Pilot Service messages

G Defunct in European waters but used in other areas for DECCA messages

H Loran messages

I Available if required

J Satnav messages

L Subfacts and Gunfacts (UK use)

V Amplifying Navigational warnings initially announced under category A

Z No messages on hand at the time

7 • BATTERIES

BATTERY TYPES

Batteries come in two basic types:

- Primary cells
- Secondary cells

Each type of battery has a number of different varieties but the main difference is that primary cells cannot be recharged, secondary cells are rechargeable.

Type of cell	Area of use
Primary cell	EPIRB, SART, Lifebuoy lights, etc
Secondary cell	Main battery, handheld VHF

Batteries have to be correctly connected into the circuit due to the terminals having either positive or negative polarity. Positive terminals should be connected to positive equipment connections and likewise with the negative terminal. Connecting the wrong way round is likely to damage both the battery and the equipment.

Primary cells

A primary cell is not rechargeable. It is filled with a variety of chemicals whose reaction is not designed to be reversible so this means that when the chemical reaction is exhausted the battery is dead. Always replace the battery with the type specified for the equipment and ensure that you regularly check these batteries for expiry dates and state of charge. Carry spares on board.

Secondary cells

These are rechargeable and are referred to as storage batteries. These are used aboard the vessel to power onboard electrical equipment such as the VHF radio and are recharged from either the vessel's engine, generator or through a battery charger connected to mains power. They come in three basic types:

- Lead acid
- Gel
- Nickel cadmium

Lead acid batteries are still the most common batteries used on boats. They have sulphuric acid for an electrolyte, and by measuring the specific gravity of the electrolyte you can accurately determine the state of charge of the battery. The specific gravity of a fully charged battery will be 1260–1290 and a discharged battery about 1160. To measure the specific gravity you use a hydrometer. A rule of thumb with the type that is colour coded is that if the float is in the green the battery is OK and if it's in the red it needs charging.

With sealed batteries the only way you can determine their state of charge is to measure the terminal voltage. Fully charged it should read 12.6 volts.

BATTERY CARE AND MAINTENANCE

1 Batteries are heavy so ensure that your battery bank is adequately secured. In the event of a knockdown you do not want the battery to get loose and become a lethal missile to the crew or for it to punch a hole in the side of the vessel.

2 House the battery in a purpose designed battery box that will allow the flammable hydrogen gas to escape but not allow sea water to get in.

3 Regularly check the electrolyte level and top up to 5mm above the plates with distilled water as required.

4 During the charging cycle, when hydrogen gas is given off, ventilate the area well and don't smoke.

5 Try to fit vents that will not allow battery acid to pour out if the boat gets caught out in a rough sea.

6 On a routine basis check for signs of corrosion and ensure that the top of the battery is kept clean. This will prevent stray currents flowing between the terminals and flattening the battery.

7 Smear a layer of petroleum jelly over the terminals to protect them from corrosion.

8 If you carry a handheld VHF ensure that you always have a fully charged spare battery on board, perhaps kept in the grab-bag. If possible buy equipment that can accept alkaline cells as these can be kept on board for extended periods and will be fully charged when needed.

9 Battery acid is corrosive so wear gloves, old clothing and eye protection when working on the battery.

The vessel's service batteries are usually kept in the bilge where the weight is low down. This makes them very vulnerable if the boat floods or catches fire and it is just these circumstances that will require a call for help. Without the battery the radio will not work so there is an argument for having a dedicated radio battery higher up in the vessel where it is more protected.

Remember that the radio relies on a battery that relies on an alternator that relies on an engine that relies on clean fuel, suitable water and regular maintenance. Ignore any part of the system at your peril!

BATTERIES

8 • THE RADIO SIGNAL

RANGE

To get the maximum range from your radio installation you will need to buy the best quality antenna, cable and connectors you can afford. Choosing the right VHF antenna is an important decision and one that requires expert advice from a reputable antenna supplier. Good transmitting antennas are usually good receiving antennas but that is not necessarily true the other way round. If the transmitter has an output of 25 watts, the aim must be to radiate the full 25 watts from the antenna. The antenna must be placed as high up as possible to get the best line of sight, (see below). On a sailing vessel it is normally a mistake to site a VHF antenna anywhere other than at the top of the mast, as lower down rigging and other structures may obscure radio signals on certain relative bearings. Powerboats generally use whip antennas but they must be mounted in the upright position.

Do not rake the antenna back, as you will lose up to 40 per cent of the antenna's radiating power.

Line of sight

VHF radio waves are like light rays, they travel in straight lines. This is why VHF is often described as a line of sight form of propagation and, just as rays of light from a lighthouse are restricted by the curvature of the earth, so are VHF radio waves. Consequently, the higher the antenna, the further over the horizon it can see. A rough rule of thumb is that for:

- Ship to ship communications the range is 10–15 miles.
- Ship to shore 30–50 miles.

If you want to calculate the distance of the radio horizon of your vessel or indeed any other antenna, you need to apply this formula:

32

Distance in nautical miles = 2.25 x sq root of height of the antenna.

It's not as daunting as it looks. Take a look at these examples:

Example 1 Your antenna height is 16m above sea level. Therefore:

$$\text{Distance in nautical miles} = 2.25 \times \sqrt{16}$$
$$= 2.25 \times 4$$
$$= 9 \text{ miles}$$

When speaking to someone in a liferaft at sea level your radio range would be about 9 miles.

Example 2 Now suppose that you are speaking to another boat with the same antenna height as your own boat. Your radio horizon would be 9 miles and so would his, so the radio range is 18 miles.

Example 3 Now suppose that you are speaking to a coast station whose antenna is 225m above sea level. His radio horizon is:

$$\text{Distance in nautical miles} = 2.25 \times \sqrt{225}$$
$$= 2.25 \times 15$$
$$= 34 \text{ miles}$$

Add to this your radio horizon of 9 miles and the total is 43 miles.
    If you don't like sums, below is a table of antenna heights and radio horizons.

Antenna height Metres	Radio horizon Miles	Antenna height Metres	Radio horizon Miles
2	3	18	9.5
4	4.5	20	10
6	5.5	22	10.5
8	6.5	24	11
10	7	26	11.5
12	8	28	12
14	8.5	30	12.5
16	9	32	13

THE RADIO SIGNAL

Digital signals are more efficient than voice (analogue) signals and so will almost always travel to the limit of the radio horizon, whereas analogue signals often fade away before they reach the radio horizon. Given the same set of circumstances, digital signals will travel between 10-20 per cent further than analogue.

High power of 25 watts will give the signal sufficient strength to reach the limit of the radio horizon, as will one watt; 25 watts simply overcomes the losses in the system caused by a less than perfect installation and ensures that the signal reaches its destination. The downside though is that the higher the power output the more battery power is required. This is why portable radios only have a limited high power of 5-6 watts because the available battery power of a portable is relatively small.

 When using a portable radio, always have a fully charged spare battery available.

One problem encountered when using a mixture of digital and analogue signals to stations over 25-30 miles away is that the digital signal will probably be received but when the signal changes to analogue, there's every chance that the signal will be lost.

The radio wave can be affected by atmospheric conditions that make it possible to hear coast stations up to 150 miles away.

EMERGENCY ANTENNA

All sailing vessels should have the VHF antenna fitted to the masthead to get the greatest possible radio range. The one drawback is in a dismasting, when the crew will lose the means to call for help. Equally, accidents can happen on a power vessel that could lead to the loss of the antenna, so it is important for all vessels to carry an emergency antenna that can be fitted to the pushpit onto a high point on the flybridge.

There is a strong argument for vessels with a fixed radio to carry a handheld VHF radio as an emergency back-up, which can be taken into the liferaft if the mother-ship is abandoned. In emergencies such

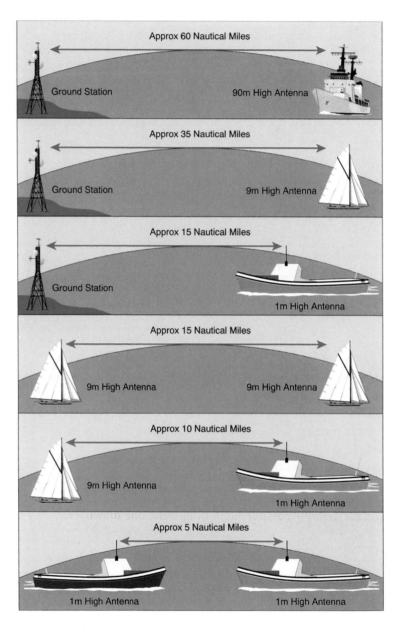

Typical VHF ranges

as grounding or a fire, the ship's battery is often the first casualty and without it the radio will not work. This is where a handheld radio is valuable, provided its battery is kept charged and the vessel always carries a fully charged spare. It should be remembered that the reduced antenna height of a portable radio and its limited high power will shorten the radio range.

CAPTURE EFFECT

When your radio is not being used as a transmitter, it is simply a receiver and it will lock on to the strongest signal it receives. This is known as the Capture Effect and it is for this reason that two power levels are available on every VHF radio. Unless you are in distress or talking to a coast station you should use the lowest power that will allow communication to take place. Imagine two boats, one mile apart, communicating on one watt. Another vessel one mile away comes onto the same channel using 25 watts. The result is that the high power signal obliterates the low power signal and this thoughtless use of the radio causes annoyance and frustration for all concerned. If you try on one watt first, but are unsuccessful, then you may try 25 watts, but please monitor the channel first to make sure it is clear.

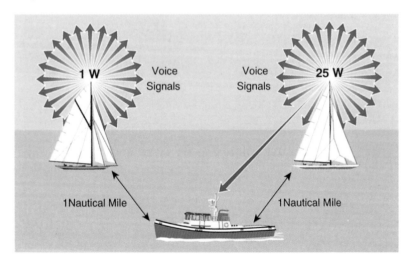

The Capture Effect

RADIO CHECK

Voice channels: It is prudent to check that the vessel's radio is in full working order whenever the vessel sets out to sea. Traditionally, we have been encouraged to call the Coastguard and ask for a 'Radio Check' which means, 'What is the strength and clarity of my transmission?'. It is classed as a test call and as such can take no longer than ten seconds.

Calling the Coastguard was no problem in the early days of marine VHF radio, when there were few leisure craft on the water. Today it is an entirely different matter. Many parts of the coast are saturated with small boats, for example, between Selsey Bill and Poole there are in excess of 50,000 boats, most with a VHF radio. If even five per cent of these vessels were out at one time, Solent Coastguard would have to deal with 2,500 radio checks. In crowded areas the advice is to check your radio by calling another vessel on an intership channel (not channel 16 please), or speaking to the Marina Control. If you get a reply, then the radio is working. If you do not use the words 'Radio Check', it is not classed as a test call, so the ten second rule does not apply. Should you need to check that CH16 is working, the Coastguard will help you with a Radio Check at any time. Solent Coastguard ask that radio check requests are made using CH67.

Digital Selective Calling Controller: Facilities may be provided within the radio under 'Other' in the Safety and Calling menu to test the DSC Controller's internal functions, without emitting a signal. Please follow the manufacturer's instructions in your radio handbook.

UNDER NO CIRCUMSTANCES SHOULD YOU TEST THE CONTROLLER BY TRANSMITTING A LIVE DISTRESS ALERT.

To test CH70 send a DSC call to another vessel and if you get a reply on an intership channel you know it works.

To test the DSC Controller, call another vessel by DSC. If you get a reply, the DSC Controller is working

THE RADIO SIGNAL

9 • INTERNATIONAL MARITIME VHF CHANNELS

CHANNEL NUMBERING

The VHF frequencies between 156.00MHz and 162.00MHz are allocated by international agreement for the Maritime Mobile Service, in other words, boats on the sea. When you purchase a Marine VHF radio, these frequencies have already been converted into numbered channels and programmed into the unit so all you need to do is select a channel.

Until 1972 there were only 28 channels but the improvements in technology then allowed those channels to be doubled by halving their frequency span. Additional channel numbers were interleaved between existing channels, but as the numbers between 29 and 59 had been allocated to other services, 60 to 88 were used instead.

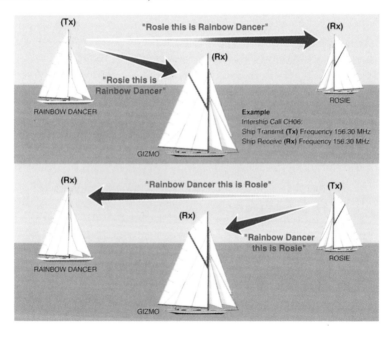

Single frequency working

Some radios are fitted with both the International Channel numbering system and the channel system used by the USA. They are very different and when you purchase your radio you should check that the International system is selected on your radio.

SINGLE FREQUENCY OR SIMPLEX CHANNELS

Single frequency channels use the same frequency for transmitting and receiving, for example CH06, the primary intership channel uses 156.30MHz. When you push the press-to-transmit button the radio transmits on that frequency and you speak. When you release the PTT switch the radio switches to receive **on the same frequency** and you listen. You can hear both sides of a conversation if both transmitters are within range because your radio is receiving on the other station's transmitting frequency.

DUAL FREQUENCY OR DUPLEX CHANNELS

Dual frequency or 'Duplex' channels use two frequencies, one to transmit a signal and one to receive a signal eg CH80, a marina working channel. This has a ship transmitting frequency of 156.025MHz and a receiving frequency of 161.625MHz. The marina will receive on 156.025 and transmit on 161.625. The advantage of a Duplex channel is that transmission is possible simultaneously in both directions. This requires a Duplex radio and two antennas, or a special duplex filter in the equipment. With this facility normal two-way conversations can be held in the same way as a normal telephone conversation because, when one antenna is transmitting the other is receiving. Because of the risk of damaging the receiver, the antennas must be far apart, preferably at either end of a ship. Another vessel close by, fitted with the same equipment will be able to hear both sides of a conversation.

INT MARITIME
VHF CHANNELS

SEMI-DUPLEX WORKING

Using two antennas is not practical on a small vessel, so most leisure craft use a semi-Duplex radio. This set-up uses one antenna to switch between two frequencies, one to transmit and one to receive. As a

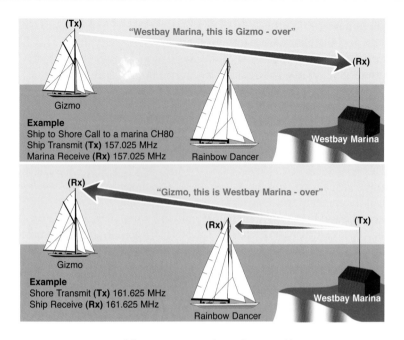

Dual frequency semi-Duplex working

consequence your radio will only ever hear on its receive frequency, in this case 161.625, a marina's transmit frequency. Another vessel close-by, fitted with a semi-Duplex radio will also only hear the marina's half of the conversation.

You will never hear the other vessels calling a marina, which is something to be aware of when calling a busy marina.

CHANNEL ALLOCATION

Each channel is allocated for one or more of the following purposes:

- Distress, Urgency, Safety
- Digital Selective Calling
- Intership
- Coast Radio Stations
- Port operations
- Ship movement
- Yacht safety (UK only)

VHF CHANNEL USAGE – AN OVERVIEW

Channels 06, 10, 67, 73
These channels have been set aside internationally for use in co-ordinated Search and Rescue operations. In the UK, their use is co-ordinated with HM Coastguard as follows:

Channel 06
Under GMDSS usage this channel is used for communications between ships and aircraft for co-ordinating Search and Rescue operations. It is also an intership working channel.

Channel 10
In addition to its use in SAR operations, this channel is used during oil spill and other pollution incidents. It is also used for the broadcast of Marine Safety Information in the UK only.

Channel 67
UK Small Craft Safety. This is also used primarily for SAR operations and for safety communications with HM Coastguard.

Channel 73
This is also used primarily for SAR operations and for the broadcast of Marine Safety Information in the UK.

Channel 13
Used for ship to ship communication relating to safety of navigation. Large vessels should monitor this channel in confined waters.

Channel 16
Used for Distress, Urgency and Safety traffic by voice. CH16 is also the intership calling channel where one of the vessels does not have DSC or where the MMSI of the called vessel is not known. It may also be used by aircraft for safety purposes.

Channel 70
Allows Digital Selective Calling for Distress, Urgency and Safety alerting in addition to initiating routine calls of other vessels and coast stations using DSC. You will need to know the MMSI of the station you wish to call.

INT MARITIME VHF CHANNELS

Channel 8, 72, 77
Used for Simplex intership communications.

Channel 80
Channel 80 is an international maritime channel allocated for use by marinas in the UK. Please note that it is a dual frequency channel.

PRIVATE CHANNELS

In addition to the International channels, there are channels available to allow communication with Private Radio stations that have to pay to use them. They are not included on the International VHF Bandplan because they are only for use in this country. The channels are:

Channels M (157.85MHz) and M2(161.425MHz)
These are UK channels and should only be used in UK territorial waters. They are generally used by yacht clubs to control club safety boats and maintain contact between a committee boat and the shore during a regatta.

QUIZ 1 • 30 QUESTIONS

1   How often must a ship station licence be renewed?

2   Under whose control may members of the crew use the VHF on board a vessel?

3   How many numbers make up an MMSI number?

4   To what do the letters MMSI refer?

5   What is a vessel's callsign?

6   To what do the letters DSC refer?

7   To what do the letters GMDSS refer?

8   Is position and time included in all DSC calls?

9   How often should the position be updated when you have to input it manually into the DSC Controller?

10   With what number must a group MMSI start?

11   What is the maximum power output of a VHF radio for use in UK vessels?

12   What does the dual watch facility allow?

13   What function does the squelch control have?

14   On which frequency is local-area Navtex transmitted?

15   On what frequency does a satellite EPIRB transmit?

16   Is it permitted to use a SART except in an emergency situation?

17   On a vessel with an antenna height of 10m and a power output of 25 watts contacting a Coast Radio Station with an antenna height of 100m, what is the likely radio range?

18   Two vessels transmit simultaneously on the same VHF channel. Vessel A is using 25 watts and vessel B is using one watt. Whose signal would another vessel, equidistant from both receive, the signal from A or B?

QUIZ 1 • 30 QUESTIONS

19 What is the maximum permitted time for a Radio Check?

20 Is it permitted to check that the radio is working by transmitting a Distress Alert on CH70?

21 What is the likely range of an intership call on full power? In the case of Distress, Urgency or Safety working, should you always use the highest or lowest power level that allows communication to take place?

23 What is a single frequency channel?

24 What is a dual frequency channel?

25 Can you use speech on CH70?

26 What is the maximum duration of a call on CH16 except in Distress and Urgency working?

27 When using CH16 for Distress, Urgency or Safety traffic, what power level should be selected, 25W or 1W?

28 When you press the PTT switch does the radio become a transmitter or receiver?

29 On which frequency is worldwide Navtex transmitted?

30 Which of the following Navtex messages can you de-select on your receiver:
- Navigational warnings
- Meteorological warnings
- Loran messages
- Search and rescue information.

Answers on pages 45–46.

QUIZ 1 • ANSWERS

1 Annually.

2 The person with the Authority To Operate.

3 9.

4 Maritime Mobile Service Identity. It is the 9-digit number used by the DSC Controller.

5 The unique number issued by Licensing Authority when a Ship Radio Licence is first issued.

6 Digital Selective Calling.

7 Global Maritime Distress and Safety System.

8 No, only Distress Alerts.

9 Regularly. Hourly if possible but at least every four hours.

10 Zero.

11 25 watts.

12 It allows you to monitor CH16 and one other channel at the same time.

13 It reduces background interference.

14 490kHz.

15 406MHz.

16 No.

17 30–40 miles.

18 A.

QUIZ 1 • ANSWERS

19 10 seconds.

20 No.

21 10 miles.

22 Lowest.

23 A channel that uses the same frequency for transmitting and receiving a signal.

24 A channel that uses one frequency for transmitting a signal and another for receiving a signal.

25 No.

26 One minute.

27 25 watts.

28 Transmitter.

29 518kHz.

30 Loran messages.

• PART 2 •
RADIO PRACTICE

10 • STANDARD PROCEDURE

REQUIREMENT FOR STANDARD PROCEDURE

English is the recognised international language of radiotelephony – thank goodness! If it were a lesser-known dialect of Outer Mongolian, or even French, most of us Anglophiles would have a severe problem. So put yourselves in the shoes of those whose first language isn't English and imagine their problems. This is why we need to use standard procedure.

Standard procedure and familiar words provide a common pattern, understood by radio operators and most nationalities. When standard words or phrases are used in an expected order, they are much easier to discern against a background of interference and poor accents. Departures from the standard procedure often create confusion, reducing the reliability and speed of communication.

To sound like a professional – learn the correct procedure.

Position

Latitude and longitude: When latitude and longitude are used they are expressed in degrees, minutes and tenths of a minute, North or South of the equator and East or West of the Greenwich Meridian. Latitude is expressed first, longitude second e.g. 50° 41' N 001° 03' W. Some vessels operate close to the Greenwich Meridian so it is vital that the radio operator knows whether he is to the East or West of it. A mistake could result in rescue services searching for a distressed vessel in the wrong area.

Example: 'There are dredging operations in position five zero degrees four one minutes North, zero one degrees zero three minutes West'.

Bearing and range: Where position is related to a charted object, the object should be well-defined, eg a lighthouse rather than a buoy. The bearing given must be in three-figure notation from true north. Also it must be the bearing that the vessel bears **from** the **charted object** not what the object bears from the vessel and so is the opposite of a waypoint's position on a GPS.

Example: 'There are sea defence operations in position two seven zero degrees from Hurst Castle, half a mile'.

Course: Course must always be given in three-figure notation from true north so an easterly course will be 090°(T) not 90°(T). Whether this is to or from a mark can be stated.

Example: 'My course is two five zero degrees true'.

Distance: Distance should be expressed in nautical miles and tenths of a mile (a cable). It is permissible to use kilometres and metres but whatever the unit it must always be stated.

Speed: Speed is expressed in knots (one knot = one nautical mile per hour). Unless stated, it indicates speed through the water and is the speed you read from your vessel's log. If you mean speed over the ground then this must be stated as 'ground speed'.

Geographical names: Place names should be those used on charts and in sailing directions. Where there is a risk of confusion, use a latitude/longitude position as confirmation.

Time: Times should be expressed using the 24 hour clock, indicating whether you are using UTC (GMT), zone time or local time.

THE PHONETIC ALPHABET

The phonetic alphabet, set out below, has been worked out by an international committee as being the most suitable words for pronunciation by radio operators of different nationalities and accents. For example, there are no words that contain 'TH' as this is very difficult for some nationalities to pronounce. It is recommended by the ITU for use in radiotelephony.

Letter	Word	Spoken as	Letter	Word	Spoken as
A	ALFA	**ALF**AH	N	NOVEMBER	NO**VEM**BER
B	BRAVO	**BRAH**VOH	O	OSCAR	**OSS**CAR
C	CHARLIE	**CHAR**LEE	P	PAPA	PAH**PAH**
D	DELTA	**DELL**TAH	Q	QUEBEC	KEH**BECK**
E	ECHO	**ECK**OH	R	ROMEO	**ROW**MEOH
F	FOXTROT	**FOK**STROT	S	SIERRA	SEE**AIR**RAH
G	GOLF	GOLF	T	TANGO	**TAN**GO
H	HOTEL	HOH**TELL**	U	UNIFORM	**YOU**NEEFORM
I	INDIA	**IN**DEEAH	V	VICTOR	**VIK**TAH
J	JULIET	**JEW**LEE**ETT**	W	WHISKEY	**WISS**KEY
K	KILO	**KEY**LOH	X	X-RAY	**ECKS**RAY
L	LIMA	**LEE**MAH	Y	YANKEE	**YANG**KEY
M	MIKE	MIKE	Z	ZULU	**ZOO**LOO

The syllables in bold type are to be emphasised. This leads to the standard pronunciation of each word.

Words that are difficult to understand, words with difficult spellings or groups of letters within the text of a message may be spelt using the phonetic alphabet. To warn the other station that you are about to spell the last word or group of words phonetically you use the words 'I Spell'. Incidentally, if you have the opportunity to name a vessel, name it with the radio in mind. Unusual spellings like *Hoof Hearted*, *Llamedos* or *Werdehelarewee* may seem like divine inspiration after a few pints, but these names will have you spelling phonetically on every radio call. Names such as *Don't Know*, *Can't Tell* or *Sinking Fast* may cause confusion to a Coastguard anxious for information and a simple name like *Ho* when repeated three times, could have you sounding like Santa. Another consideration is length. *Flame Lily of Buckler's Hard* is not only a bit of a mouthful but you'll need a lottery win for the dodger letters.

To save time and mistakes it is always a good idea to have the vessel's name and callsign spelt phonetically on a card, displayed near the radio.

Phonetic numbers

When numbers are transmitted, send them digit by digit using the following pronunciation to aid clarity:

Number	Written	Pronounced
1	ONE	WUN
2	TWO	TOO
3	THREE	TREE
4	FOUR	FOWER
5	FIVE	FIFE
6	SIX	SIX
7	SEVEN	SEV-EN
8	EIGHT	AIT
9	NINE	NINE
0	ZERO	ZERO

PRO-WORDS

These can best be described as procedural words that are used by all nationalities to avoid confusion. They are designed for brevity. Brevity was once defined as 'the soul of lingerie' ie the shorter and less there is the better. It is also the soul of radio communication.

The following list of pro-words is those that you are likely to use, so it is worth learning them:

OVER The invitation to reply to your transmission.

OUT Signifies the end of working and no reply is expected. So it is wrong to say 'over and out'.

RECEIVED Used to acknowledge the receipt of a message.

SAY AGAIN Used when you require a message or part of a message to be repeated or emphasised. Used with: ALL; WORD AFTER; WORD BEFORE; ALL AFTER; ALL BEFORE; ALL BETWEEN.

I SAY AGAIN The response to SAY AGAIN.

REPEAT This is used when emphasis is required.

RADIO CHECK Please tell me the strength and clarity of my transmission. Radio checks are classed as test calls and therefore, must take no longer than 10 seconds.

I SPELL Intention to spell the last word or group of letters phonetically.

CORRECTION Spoken during the transmission of a message indicating that an error has been made and is about to be corrected.

IN FIGURES The following numeral or group of numerals are to be written as figures.

IN LETTERS The following numeral or group of numerals are to be written in letters, ie if an address is 21 Sevenoaks Road it might get written as 217 Oaks Road.

STATION CALLING Used when a station receives a call intended for it but is uncertain of the identity of the station calling.

THIS IS This transmission is from the station whose name or callsign follows.

DELTA ECHO Where there are language difficulties it is used instead of 'This is'.

I READ BACK If the receiving station is doubtful about all or part of a message the station may repeat it back to the transmitting station. It precedes the repetition with 'I read back'.

WRONG Used by the receiving station if the above has incorrectly been repeated back.

TRANSMISSION RULES – The 14 Commandments

Transmission rules are the radio equivalent of the Ten Commandments. They are simple rules, laid down internationally and are essential to the efficient use of radio frequencies and channels. The following are strictly forbidden – you break them at your peril!

1 **Transmissions without identification.** A station's identity can either be the vessel's name, callsign or the 9-digit Maritime Mobile Service Identity (MMSI).

2 **The use of Christian names or other names in lieu of the ship's name or callsign.** No 'Ten Four Good Buddy – Come Back' or other such 'handles'.

3 **Transmissions which have not been authorised by the Master of the vessel.** The Master of the vessel must permit the radio's use but he may not necessarily be the person with the authority to operate.

4 **Operation of a VHF radio by unauthorised persons.** Calls can be made under the close supervision of a person with the authority to operate. It is the person with the authority to operate who controls the use of the radio once permission to use the radio has been received from the Master of the vessel.

5 **Transmission of false Distress, Safety or identification signals.** It is an offence to put out false signals. Regardless of how much you like watching lifeboats or want to be beamed up from your heaving vessel into a safe, stable helicopter, it is illegal. False signals that are malicious carry severe penalties. Be very careful if you have inquisitive, bored or rebellious children on board.

6 **Closing down before finishing all operations resulting from a Distress call, Urgency or Safety signal.** When you become involved in any of the situations above, lives may depend on your radio link remaining open.

7 **Broadcasting messages or programmes without expecting a reply.** The radio is licensed for communication, not broadcasting. An 'All Ships' call is not a broadcast but a message addressed to all stations listening to that channel.

8 **Making unnecessary transmissions or transmitting superfluous signals.** Unnecessary transmissions are those that are not concerned with ship's business. Superfluous signals indicate that your radio installation could be faulty and should be repaired before making further transmissions.

9 **Transmission of obscene, profane or indecent language.** Even if a vessel has forced you to give way when you were the stand-on vessel, you cannot doubt the parentage of its Master over the air.

10 **Use of frequencies other then those covered by the ship's licence.** The ship's licence only covers the vessel for the frequencies stated in it. It does not cover you for any other service eg Amateur Radio, Civil Aviation frequencies, etc.

11 **The broadcast or transmission of music.** It is not permitted to liven up the airways with a rousing sea shanty.

12 **The transmission of messages intended for reception of addresses on shore, except through a Coast Radio Station.** It is forbidden to use a marine VHF radio in place of a normal telephone but it is permissible to use CB radio, a mobile phone or, if you are a licensed radio amateur, ham radio.

13 **The broadcast of messages intended for reception of addresses on shore.** For example, the family of a fisherman has a radio scanner at home to monitor the whereabouts of the fishing vessel. The fisherman cannot broadcast to his family, 'Home in half an hour, get the coffee on for me and the lads'.

14 **Secrecy of correspondence. Radio operators and others shall not divulge the contents or even the existence of any correspondence that is transmitted, intercepted or received.**
   When you apply to be examined for your radio certificate you will be asked to sign a 'Declaration of Secrecy in the Operation of Radio Apparatus'. It says:
   'I .... do solemnly and sincerely declare that I will not improperly divulge to any person the purport of any message which I may transmit or receive by means of any radio apparatus operated by me which may come to my knowledge in connection with the operation of the said apparatus.'
   Therefore, regardless of the fee tabloid newspapers are prepared to pay for the sensational revelations received on your radio, you are bound to absolute secrecy by this section of the 1884 Post Office Protection Act.

VOICE PROCEDURE

When you first use a radiotelephone you are likely to be very nervous, especially if you are speaking to professionals such as the Coastguard. But with use, the art of communicating by voice over the radio becomes easier and you soon learn to relax. Once you have worked out what to say you have to consider how you will say it.

The necessity for clear speech over the radio is obvious, as a message that is difficult to understand is as reliable as a politician's promise. There are several points to consider:

PITCH The voice should be pitched at a slightly higher level than for normal conversation. Any tendency to drop the pitch of the voice at the end of a word or phrase should be avoided.

VOLUME The microphone should be held a couple of inches in front and to the side of the mouth. Speak into it at normal conversation level and do not shout as shouting may overload the microphone causing distortion. If the person receiving your call cannot hear you he can alter the volume at his end. It also avoids the remnants of your last meal ending up in the mesh of the microphone!

CLARITY Speak clearly, so that there can be no confusion with other words and emphasise weak syllables so that a word such as 'roar' is not mistaken for 'raw'. People with strong accents must be aware that they may not be so easily understood over the radio.

SPEECH Messages to be copied down should be sent slowly and in phrases rather than word by word. Pause at the end of each phrase to allow the receiving operator to copy it down and remember that the average reading speed is 250 words a minute, speaking speed is 150 words a minute and writing speed is only 20 words a minute. Any Radio 4 Shipping Forecast announcers reading this please take note.

To avoid too many 'ums and errs', write down exactly what you want to say. It will give you confidence and save time.

11 • CALLS AND CALLING

THE CALLING CHANNELS
Channel 70

Channel 70 uses only digital communications. it is used for digital alerts that are to do with Distress, Urgency and Safety, or when an MMSI number is used to contact another vessel or shoreside facility, such as the Coastguard.

This channel is automatically selected when the 'enter' or 'send' buttons are used and does not need to be selected manually, as other channels do.

Channel 70 has a capacity of around 500 calls an hour. Distress Alerts are given in a series of five consecutive calls. If the first one or two clash with other DSC traffic, the other calls will get through and it only requires one of the five to be successful.

Channel 16

Provision has been made in the GMDSS to limit CH16 to Distress, Urgency and Safety traffic. However, until the majority of vessels have DSC, or the UK authorities allocate an alternative non-DSC calling channel, CH16 can be used for intership calling in addition to Distress, Urgency and Safety working. Therefore the use of CH16 broadly falls into two main categories:

1 **Distress, Urgency and Safety traffic on radiotelephony.** Once the initial Distress, Urgency or Safety Alert has been transmitted on CH70 the radio automatically re-tunes to CH16 for the subsequent voice communication with the acknowledging station.

2 **The calling channel.** For vessels that do not have a DSC radio or where a vessel's MMSI number is unknown, CH16 acts as a meeting place for intership calls prior to changing to a working channel. Vessels with a DSC radio will use CH70 as the calling channel except for organisations that must be contacted directly by voice on their

working channels. Always check the working channel with *Reeds Nautical Almanac* or the *Admiralty List of Radio Signals*.

To assist in the reception of Distress traffic, no transmissions on CH16 should exceed one minute. This highlights one of the fundamental differences between using CH70 and CH16 for calling. Using CH70 the digital call is virtually instantaneous.

If the DSC Controller has selected CH16 for Distress, Urgency or Safety traffic, or you have pressed the CH16 dedicated button, high power will be automatically selected. If you are about to make a call where high power is not required, select low power.

When monitoring in dual watch and a signal is detected on CH16, the receiver will remain on CH16 for the duration of the call. When a signal is detected on the alternate channel, CH16 will continue to be sampled at intervals for a fraction of a second, interrupting reception on the channel in use. If a signal is detected on CH16, the receiver will lock onto it and communications with the alternate channel will be lost.

INITIAL CALLS BY RADIOTELEPHONE (VOICE)

All calls on the radio follow the same pattern and conform to standard radio procedure.

Before making the call always check the channel is clear.

Every initial call on the radiotelephone has four components:

1 THE IDENTITY OF THE STATION CALLED

This is the vessel's name, callsign or 9-digit MMSI number. For DSC transmissions you will use the MMSI number, for voice transmissions you will normally use the vessel's name. However, where there are two vessels bearing the same name or there is a risk of confusion, such as being unable to pronounce the vessel's name, you will use the vessel's callsign or its MMSI number. The spoken repetition of identity is between one and three times and dependent on a variety of factors:

● Is the station expecting a call or are you calling on a working channel? If so the radio operator will be tuned in to listen for the vessel's identity so one call only is needed.

● Is the vessel likely to be monitoring the channel, but not be expecting a call? In this case it would be better to call twice, once to alert, the second to confirm.

- Are radio conditions difficult or are you involved with Distress, Urgency or Safety working? In this case you must call three times.

2 THE WORDS *THIS IS* FOLLOWED BY –

3 THE IDENTITY OF THE CALLING STATION
This is the vessel's name, callsign or 9-digit MMSI number. Again the spoken repetition of identity depends on a variety of factors.

- Is the station likely to be monitoring the channel, but not be expecting a call? In this case it would be better to call twice as the second call will confirm the calling station's identity.
- Are radio conditions difficult or are you involved with Distress, Urgency or Safety working? In this case you must call three times.

4 AN INVITATION TO REPLY
The word 'over'. After contact is established, the callsign or other identification need only be transmitted once on each 'over'.

CONTROL OF COMMUNICATIONS

Ship to shore

When talking to coast stations, regardless of who starts the conversation, it is the coast station that controls communications by giving you the working channel to use. This is because they are only licensed for the channels they are permitted to use, eg the Coastguard will have CH16, 67 and so forth. The same will apply to DSC. When you have entered the MMSI of the coast station you wish to call, the DSC Controller will not ask you to enter a working channel, instead the ship's radio will automatically tune to the working channel indicated in the DSC acknowledgement.

Intership

In intership communication on DSC, it is the calling vessel that chooses the intership channel. If this is inconvenient for the receiving station he has two choices. The first is to make a fresh DSC call back to the calling station suggesting an alternative channel, or secondly, he can suggest the alternative channel when the communication goes over to voice on

CALLS AND CALLING

the first suggested intership channel. The called vessel therefore still controls communications.

When using CH16 for the initial call it is now recommended that the calling station nominates an empty channel as it makes the use of CH16 more efficient. But be aware that not all ship stations have the full number of channels available so the called station needs to agree to a suggested channel. Some portable radios have a very limited number of channels. In all cases the called station controls communication.

When calling on CH16, it is a good idea to suggest a working channel in the first 'Over'. It saves time on CH16 but does not override the called station's right to control the communication.

Watchkeeping

The VHF radio has two receivers: one that constantly monitors CH70 and another that monitors a channel of your choice, ideally, this should be CH16. It must be remembered that because there is only one antenna, watchkeeping on CH70 is suspended when the radio is transmitting. With dual watch selected, it is possible to monitor a third channel. In confined waters large vessels should monitor CH13, which is allocated for bridge to bridge safety. Consequently, it is recommended that all vessels monitor CH16 and CH13 when they encounter shipping close to major ports.

When a ship station receives a message on CH70 an alarm will sound and the message will be displayed on the display screen. Once the receiving operator has accepted the call, the DSC Controller will automatically switch the radio to the suggested channel contained in the message. Calls are also logged and stored for later retrieval.

Another aspect of good watchkeeping is the ability of the skipper to monitor the radio as well as what is happening on deck by having a waterproof extension speaker in the cockpit. This is especially useful in rescue situations where the skipper is required to be everywhere at once. With a speaker in the cockpit a member of the crew can be detailed below to take instructions from the lifeboat or helicopter on the main radio while the skipper keeps control of the activities on deck.

If you fit an external speaker, do not install it next to the steering compass. The magnets in the speaker may induce deviation.

Garbled calls

There are two common types of garbled calls. They are:

1 STATION CALLED – CALLSIGN GARBLED
When a station receives a call without being certain that it is intended for it, it **must not reply**. It must wait until the call has been repeated and understood otherwise if all the listening stations replied, there would be chaos.

2 CALLING STATION – CALLSIGN GARBLED
When a station receives a call, which is intended for it, but is uncertain of the calling station's identity, it should reply as follows:

STATION CALLING GIZMO – STATION CALLING GIZMO – THIS IS GIZMO – SAY AGAIN – OVER.

Unanswered calls

Voice
Continued repeated calls are a frequent unnecessary use of a channel and a pain to everyone listening. If a call goes unanswered check that the controls on your set are correctly adjusted.

Install the radio where the controls can be easily used and read.

Check that
- The power is on.
- You have selected high power if you have been using low power.
- The volume is turned up. The station may be replying but with the volume turned down you will not hear it.

- Squelch is adjusted to cut out background noise only and not the incoming signal.
- The correct channel is selected. Are you in dual watch mode?

You may repeat the call at two-minute intervals up to a maximum of three consecutive calls. After this a three-minute gap should elapse before trying again. This does not apply to Distress working.

Unanswered calls – DSC

All calls by DSC are stored under the RECEIVED CALLS or LOG menu for retrieval later. As a minimum the DSC Controller must be able to store details of the last call received. To check your logged calls choose RECEIVED CALLS and scroll through the list.

PRE-CALL PROFORMA

Before you make any call on the radio you need to assemble all the information that will be required. Most small craft operators do not use the radio sufficiently for all the procedures to become second nature, so I suggest you try using a pre-call proforma like this 'Calling Card' opposite.

Laminate the card so that it is re-usable. Before laminating, fill in the vessel's name, callsign and phonetic spelling in permanent ink. The variable information can be added using a dry-wipe pen or Chinagraph pencil.

CALLING CARD

CHANNEL FOR INITIAL CALL:	CHANNEL FOR MESSAGE:
CALLED STATION IDENTITY:	MMSI:
NAME:	CALLSIGN:
CALLING STATION IDENTITY:	MMSI:
NAME:	

PHONETIC SPELLING:

CALLSIGN PHONETICS:

INFORMATION TO BE INCLUDED IN THE MESSAGE:

© SUE FLETCHER 2005

Using a Calling Card for a marina call

CALLING CARD

CHANNEL FOR INITIAL CALL: **80**	CHANNEL FOR MESSAGE: **80**
CALLED STATION IDENTITY:	MMSI:
NAME: **WESTBAY MARINA**	CALLSIGN:
CALLING STATION IDENTITY:	
NAME: **RAINBOW DANCER**	

PHONETIC SPELLING:
**ROMEO, ALPHA, INDIA, NOVEMBER, BRAVO, OSCAR, WHISKEY
DELTA, ALPHA, NOVEMBER, CHARLEE, ECHO, ROMEO**

CALLSIGN PHONETICS:
MIKE, ZULU, MIKE, SIERRA, SIX

INFORMATION TO BE INCLUDED IN THE MESSAGE:
Want a berth for 4 nights with a shore power connection
Length: 14.25M   *Draught*: 2M   *Beam*: 3.3M

© SUE FLETCHER 2005

CALLS AND CALLING

12 • INTERSHIP WORKING

INTERSHIP CHANNELS

Channel no	Single frequency	Ship transmit	Ship receive
6	✔	156.300	156.300
8	✔	156.400	156.400
72	✔	156.625	156.625
77	✔	156.875	156.875

Intership channels are not for 'chatting' between ships but are for passing messages concerned with ship's business. What exactly constitutes ship's business is hard to define. A discussion about your favourite TV soap is definitely not ship's business, whilst a recommendation to use Bogogloop for your leaking stern gland probably is. Although no one is going to object to a few pleasantries, never forget that all the time you have the PTT switch depressed, you are monopolising that channel and everyone else tuned into the channel can hear you.

Channels 6, 8, 72 and 77 are exclusively for intership use and all radios must be fitted with Channel 6, the primary intership channel. Each channel is single frequency. This means that other vessels tuned into the same channel can hear both sides of your conversation. If you are not using DSC to make the initial call, you will have to choose the intership channel on which you will pass your message. Because of the pressure placed on this limited number of channels use higher numbered channels where possible. We are conditioned to start with the lowest channel number and work up until a free channel is located. If you want a free channel try starting with the highest numbered channel and work down. It is not essential to use CH16 for the initial call as you can arrange to call direct on an intership channel.

COLLISION AVOIDANCE

It is often assumed that a VHF radio is a useful aid to collision avoidance because it allows two vessels to speak to each other. This must be treated with caution for four reasons:

1 You may be able to identify the name of a ship but is he able to identify you? From his bridge he is likely to be able to see several small boats and from a distance one yacht or powerboat looks like another. Can you be sure that he knows with which vessel he is making collision avoidance arrangements? Often, by the time it becomes obvious that a mistake has been made, it is too late to avoid a collision.

2 Collision regulations. Under the rules of the road, vessels less than 20m long must not impede the safe passage of vessels that can only navigate in a deep-water channel. So don't bother with the radio – obey the rules.

3 High-speed commercial traffic, with its tight timetables and business pressures, is relying increasingly on navigation aids with the consequence of less time to discuss arrangements for collision avoidance. In poor visibility you may get your first sighting of a fast ferry when it is only one mile away and with a closing speed of 45 knots you will have a little over one minute to decide what to do.

4 Unless you know the MMSI number of the vessel you will have to call on CH16 or CH13. In open sea, with vessels using automatic watch-keeping by DSC on CH70, calls made on CH16 may go unheard.

In open water, monitor CH16 and CH13 in dual watch. The other vessel may try to contact you.

ONBOARD COMMUNICATIONS

Onboard communications using handheld equipment should be carried out using channels 15 and 17, as they are automatically restricted to a power output of one watt to prevent interference on CH16. The usual format of an onboard call is to refer to the fixed radio as 'Vessel name control' and each transportable radio as 'Vessel name Alfa, Bravo, Charlie ' and so on. For example:

'Gizmo Alfa, this is Gizmo Control, over'.

HOW TO MAKE A DSC INTERSHIP CALL

Note that all sets are slightly different.
For this call you must know the MMSI of the station you wish to call.

Press the MENU or CALL button – the Controller will
display the Safety and Calling menu.

Press SCROLL to bring
INDIVIDUAL CALL onto the screen.

INDIVIDUAL CALL:

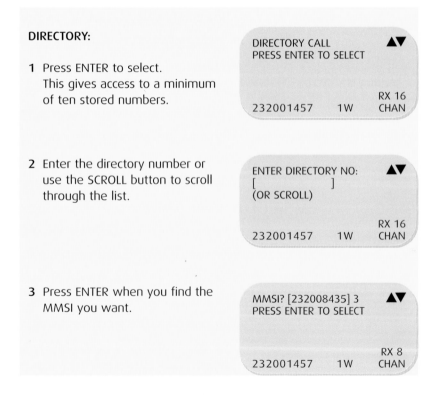

Using the SCROLL button you will be offered the sub-menu:

DIRECTORY:

1 Press ENTER to select.
  This gives access to a minimum
  of ten stored numbers.

2 Enter the directory number or
  use the SCROLL button to scroll
  through the list.

3 Press ENTER when you find the
  MMSI you want.

4 The Controller will suggest a working channel.

5 If this is not the channel you want SCROLL until it appears.

CHANNEL? 6
PRESS ENTER TO SELECT

RX 6
232001457   1W   CHAN

6 Press ENTER when you have the correct channel on the screen.

7 Press ENTER to send.

CHANNEL? 6
PRESS ENTER TO SEND

RX 6
232001457   1W   CHAN

8 The radio will then re-tune to the working channel.

Manual

1 This option invites you to enter an MMSI manually through the numeric keypad.

MANUAL MMS1? [   ]

RX 16
232001457   1W   CHAN

2 Using the numeric keypad enter the MMSI number.

3 Press ENTER.

MANUAL MMS1? [232001456]

PRESS ENTER TO SELECT

RX 16
232001457   1W   CHAN

4 The Controller will suggest a working channel.

5 If this is not acceptable SCROLL for an alternative.

CHANNEL? 6
PRESS ENTER TO SELECT

RX 6
232001457   1W   CHAN

6 Press ENTER to select.

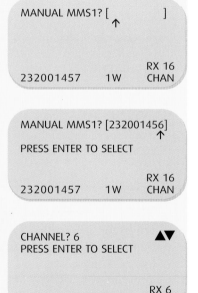

INTERSHIP WORKING

7 Press ENTER to send.

8 The radio will re-tune to the
   working channel.

> MMS1 [232001456] CHANNEL 72
> PRESS ENTER TO SEND
>
>   RX 72
> 232001457   1W   CHAN

Keep a record of MMSI numbers and vessel names.

RESPONDING TO A DSC INTERSHIP CALL

Just as a telephone rings when a call is received, your radio will sound
an alarm and display the call details.

1 When a call is received, the screen
   will show the MMSI of the calling
   station and suggested working
   channel.

2 Press ENTER to answer the call.

> CALL FROM 232005472 ON CH77
> PRESS ENTER TO ANSWER
>
>   RX 77
> 232001457   1W   CHAN

3 The radio will automatically re-tune to the working channel.

If the suggested channel is inconvenient you have two options.

● **Option 1** is to send a DSC call back to the calling station with the
  working channel number to use.
● **Option 2** Ask the calling station to change to your chosen channel.

The called vessel must start the conversation on the selected intership
channel. Your vessel's name is *Rosie* and the call will start like this:

STATION CALLING ROSIE
THIS IS ROSIE
OVER

An example of an intership call using DSC

Rainbow Dancer calls Rosie by DSC.   Rosie receives the DCS call.

CHANNEL ? 77   ▲▼
PRESS ENTER TO SEND
RX 77
232001457   1W   CHAN

CALL FROM [232001457] ON CH77
PRESS ENTER TO ANSWER
RX 77
232000763   1W   CHAN

Rosie accepts the call. Radio tunes to CH77.

Station calling Rosie
This is Rosie
OVER

Rosie, this is Rainbow Dancer
We are two miles east of
Lulworth Cove.
ETA thirty minutes.
What is your position and ETA?
OVER

Rainbow Dancer, this is Rosie
We are four miles south
west of Lulworth.
ETA one hour.
We will see you there.
OVER

Rosie, this is Rainbow Dancer
Fine, we'll have the
corkscrew ready.
Rainbow Dancer
OUT

Rosie OUT

INTERSHIP WORKING

MMSI UNKNOWN – HOW TO MAKE
AN INTERSHIP CALL (VOICE ONLY)

- Note down all the information required to make the call (See Pre-call Proforma page 63).
- Check to see which intership channel is free and note its number. Although it is the called station that controls communication, there is nothing to prevent the calling station suggesting an intership working channel. This makes sense because the calling station knows that it is about to make the call, but the called station does not. It can save time and prevent the confusion that arises if the vessel called plucks a channel number out of the air that turns out to be in use.
- Select CH16, select low power, press your PTT switch and transmit the initial call.

  Example:

  > YACHT ROSIE, YACHT ROSIE
  > THIS IS RAINBOW DANCER, RAINBOW DANCER
  > CHANNEL 77
  > OVER

- Remain on CH16 for the answer. If no answer is heard, wait two minutes and try again. Don't forget you can only try three times with a two-minute interval between. After that you must wait for three minutes.
- If the station does answer and agrees with your suggestion, re-tune the radio to CH77 and pass your message.
- The called station starts the conversation on the working channel.
- Each station must identify itself on each OVER.
- When the message has been passed, each station signs OUT. This signifies the end of working and indicates to any station waiting to use the channel that it is about to become free.

It is preferable to 'meet' directly on an intership channel to obviate the risk of losing the other station during channel changing.

13 • HM COASTGUARD

HM COASTGUARD CHANNELS

Channel	DSC calling	Voice calling	Working channel	Single frequency	Dual frequency
70	✔			✔	
16		✔		✔	
10			✔	✔	
23			✔		✔
67			✔	✔	
73			✔	✔	
84			✔		✔
86			✔		✔

COASTGUARD SERVICES

VHF radio

Her Majesty's Coastguard (HMCG) has established Maritime Rescue Co-ordination Centres and Sub-Centres all around the coastline of the UK and is responsible in the UK for the broadcast of Maritime Safety Information (MSI) on VHF, MF and Navtex and for the provision of Radio Medical Link Calls (MEDLINK) service.

MSI broadcasts include navigational warnings, meteorological warnings, SUBFACTS – submarine movements and GUNFACTS – naval gunnery activity.

The network of HMCG remote radio sites around the coast of the UK provides VHF and MF coverage out to 30 miles and 150 miles respectively, with Navtex coverage out to 270 miles.

MSI broadcasts are made using two differing routines:

Routine A broadcasts are made every four hours on VHF Channels 10, 23, 73, 84, and 86 and, exceptionally, on CH67, following an initial announcement of the appropriate working channel on CH16. This prevents mutual interference and allows one operator to broadcast simultaneously on two

71

or more antennas. This is important when some of the broadcasts take in excess of 20 minutes. The broadcast times can be found in almanacs and in the table below and times are always given in UTC.

Included in Routine A broadcasts are:

- Local inshore forecast – within 12 miles of the coast. The forecast is the Marinecall forecast, it covers 48 hours. It will give details of the wind expected; sea state; sea temperature and visibility readings around the local coast. It also advises of strong wind warnings when appropriate – force 6 and above.
- Gale warning.
- Navigational warnings.
- Gunfacts/subfacts – from selected stations only.

Routine B broadcasts consist of area weather forecasts (including shipping forecasts for adjacent sea areas and the outlook) that are transmitted twice daily at the times shown in the right hand column of the table. The stations are listed in alphabetical order.

Station name	Routine A every 4 hours from:	Routine B twice daily from:
Aberdeen	0320	0720
Belfast	0305	0705
Brixham	0050	0850
Clyde	0020	0820
Dover	0105	0905
Falmouth	0140	0940
Forth	0205	1005
Holyhead	0235	0635
Humber	0340	0740
Liverpool	0210	1010
Milford Haven	0335	0735
Portland	0220	1020
Shetland	0105	0905
Solent	0040	0840
Stornaway	0110	0910
Swansea	0005	0805
Thames	0010	0810
Yarmouth	0040	0840

The broadcast of MSI may be interrupted or delayed as a result of Search and Rescue operations.

Direction finding

Each Coastguard station is fitted with direction finding equipment. This equipment locks onto a vessel's VHF signal and, because the signal travels in a straight line, the Coastguard can home in on a vessel. The primary purpose of this equipment is to provide bearings of vessels in distress but the HMCG may be able to provide position information, using VHF direction finding to any navigator concerned about his navigational position. It must be stressed that this is a bonus not a service. Over-use would inevitably detract from its availability for distress. DO NOT ABUSE IT!

Radio checks

Radio checks are available from HMCG, but the increasing number of small craft operators can, in some areas, stretch resources to their limit. Use another vessel in preference.

Channel navigation information service

HM Coastguard provides a 24-hour radio safety service for all shipping in the Dover Strait. It is broadcast 40 minutes past every hour on VHF Channel 11 and gives warnings of navigational difficulties and unfavourable conditions likely to be encountered in the Strait. These include adverse weather conditions, exceptional tides, defective navigational aids and hampered vessels.

Small Craft Safety Scheme

The scheme involves filling in a card (CG66, available from the Coastguard, marinas, chandlers etc) with the details of your vessel, shore contact, radio equipment, lifesaving equipment and usual areas of operation. This is then logged with the Coastguard. If anxious relatives report that you are overdue at your destination or if you are unlucky enough to need rescue, the Coastguard will have a description of your vessel and equipment. Details of any major passage planned can be passed as Safety Traffic to the Coastguard on your departure from port. These details will be logged. When you arrive at your destination or diversion port you must let your shoreside contact know by telephone that you have arrived safely. The Coastguard does not have the facilities to monitor every vessel's movements so it is the responsibility of the skipper to ring home. In this way much of the time spent in looking for 'overdue' vessels can be eliminated.

The details need to be updated at least every two years otherwise your card will be withdrawn. Don't forget to update the card if you change your boat.

The Voluntary Identification Safety Scheme can give the Coastguard a good deal of information about vessels involved in incidents and hopefully speed up the Search and Rescue operation.

Safety and SOLAS V

In 1959, the newly formed International Maritime Organisation adopted the first International Convention for the Safety of Life at Sea (SOLAS) and there have been numerous updates since, including SOLAS V, which came into force on 1 July 2002.

Some parts of the latest SOLAS V regulations have been applied to all vessels, large and small, and are listed below.

Most recreational boaters meet these regulations through common sense but conforming to SOLAS regulations is extremely important. In addition to good seamanship, leisure sailors need to be aware that failing to comply is breaking the law. It could affect your insurance and you could even be prosecuted following an incident if you are found not to have complied.

Regulation V3/4: Safe navigation and avoidance of dangerous situations

This concerns passage planning and applies to all vessels that go to sea, even if that only means tidal rivers and estuaries. Whilst this may seem irrelevant, most boaters must familiarise themselves with the following:

- Weather.
- Tides.
- Limitations of the vessel.

- Crew ability and experience.
- Navigational dangers. Charts covering the area must be up-to-date and on board.
- Contingency plan in case something goes wrong.
- Someone onshore knows where you are going and what to do if they become concerned.

Regulation V29: Lifesaving signals

SOLAS states that an illustrated table of the recognised lifesaving signals should be carried and easily accessible on board. The signals are available in printed form from the MCA and are also listed in the *RYA Boat Safety Handbook* or *Reeds Nautical Almanac*. Below is a list of internationally recognised distress signals:

- A Distress Alert sent by digital means on CH70 of a VHF Digital Selective Calling radio.
- The word Mayday by voice on the radio. Mayday is derived from the French *m'aidez* – help me.
- Signals transmitted by an Emergency Position Indicating Radio Beacon (EPIRB).
- Red flares – handheld or parachute.
- Orange smoke signal.
- Continuous sounding of a foghorn.
- The signal transmitted by a Search and Rescue Radar Transponder (SART).
- Flames on a vessel.
- Slowly and repeatedly raising and lowering arms outstretched to the side.
- A ball over or under a square. The anchor ball raised above or below a flag will suffice.
- SOS by sound or light. SOS in Morse is dot-dot-dot dash-dash-dash dot-dot-dot.
- The signal code flags NC.

Regulation V/31, V/32 and V/33: Assistance to other craft
The Coastguard and any other vessels must be informed should you encounter anything that could cause a serious hazard to navigation. They must be notified by VHF or by telephone at the earliest opportunity. Any distress signal must be responded to as best you can. More on this later in the book.

Regulation V/35: Prohibition of misuse of any distress signals
An example would be transmitting a false Mayday call.

THE COASTGUARD AND VHF DSC

Each Coastguard station has been issued with an MMSI and these are detailed below in alphabetical order.

Station name	MMSI Number	Station name	MMSI Number
Aberdeen	002320004	London Coastguard	002320063
Belfast	002320021	Milford Haven	002320017
Brixham	002320013	Oban	002320023
Clyde	002320022	Portland	002320012
Dover	002320010	Shetland	002320001
Falmouth	002320014	Solent	002320011
Forth	002320005	Stornoway	002320024
Holyhead	002320018	Swansea	002320016
Humber	002320007	Thames	002320009
Liverpool	002320019	Yarmouth	002320008

If you regularly sail in an area, program the MMSI of the local Coastguard station(s) into your DSC Controller directory.

CALLING THE COASTGUARD – ROUTINE CALLS

Coastguards maintain a continuous watch on CH70 for DSC Distress, Urgency and Safety traffic. CH16 is also monitored by loudspeaker and by headset when the senior officer considers it appropriate. In the UK CH67 is reserved for small craft to speak on matters of safety direct to the Coastguard but you cannot call the Coastguard direct on that channel except in the Solent where it is requested.

Calls to the Coastguard by DSC are carried out as follows:

1 On the DSC Controller call up the Safety and Calling menu.

2 Under Individual Call, enter the MMSI of the Coastguard station into the Controller either manually or from the Directory.

3 When the Coastguard acknowledges the call he will indicate the working channel for voice communications and the radio will re-tune automatically. When you call **any** coast station by DSC the coast station will indicate the working channel.

4 On the working channel pass your message by voice.

77

DSC CONTROLLER:

1 Press MENU on the DSC Controller.
2 Scroll to INDIVIDUAL CALL.
3 Press ENTER.
4 Press MANUAL.
5 Press ENTER.
6 Enter the MMSI of the Coastguard.
7 Press ENTER.
8 Press ENTER to send call.

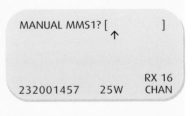

A safety traffic call using DSC

You sight a floating container and you are within radio range of the coast. You call the nearest Coastguard station to allow them to re-broadcast the safety message using their more powerful transmitter. To call the Coastguard follow this procedure:

HM COASTGUARD

The radio will automatically re-tune to CH16, or the working channel assigned in the CG acknowledgement, so that the message can be passed to the Coastguard by voice. For example:

16 Solent Coastguard, Solent Coastguard,
Solent Coastguard.
This is Rainbow Dancer,
Rainbow Dancer, Rainbow Dancer.
Call Sign MIKE ZULU MIKE SIERRA SIX.
I have safety traffic for you.
OVER

> Rainbow Dancer.
> This is Solent Coastguard.
> Go to CH67.
> OVER

67 Solent Coastguard.
This is Rainbow Dancer.
My position is 165°(T) St Catherine's
Lighthouse 6.25 NM
I have sighted a floating container
drifting East.
Approximately half a mile South East
of my position.
OVER

Request for medical advice

The skipper of any vessel requiring medical advice can contact the nearest HMCG co-ordination centre on either VHF-DSC or VHF Channel 16, requesting 'Medical Advice'. Alternatively, particularly in an urgent situation, an urgency alert using the pro-words 'Pan Pan' should be broadcast. If the condition is life threatening, a heart attack for example, a Distress Alert using the pro-word 'Mayday' should be used. More on these calls later in the book.

The co-ordination centre will give priority to requests for medical advice. A doctor from a nominated hospital will be contacted by telephone, and the doctor will be linked to the vessel through the co-ordinating centre via an appropriate VHF channel. While the call is being placed, the Coastguard will establish additional information with the vessel relating to position, a description of the vessel, and if appropriate, details of the casualty. Channels 23, 84 or 86 will invariably be used for Medical Link Calls, and, frequently, a mobile phone is used.

AVOIDING TROUBLE

Avoiding getting into trouble at sea should be the number one priority of every skipper. Below is a chart showing the typical statistical breakdown of calls for assistance. The largest percentage is for machinery failure followed by adverse weather conditions. Consequently, before setting out to sea you should:

- Ensure that everything on board is in full working order.
- That you have plenty of spares for the bits that are likely to break.
- That you know how to fit the spares.
- That you listen to the latest weather forecast (see SOLAS V)
- That you know how to get the boat and crew safely to their destination.

HM COASTGUARD

Don't become a statistic!

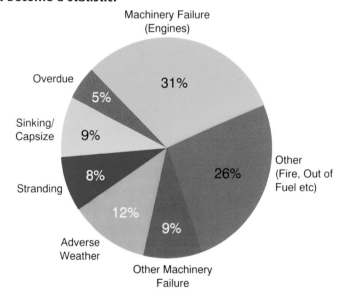

Machinery Failure (Engines) 31%

Overdue 5%

Sinking/Capsize 9%

Stranding 8%

Adverse Weather 12%

Other Machinery Failure 9%

Other (Fire, Out of Fuel etc) 26%

14 • Port Operations and Harbour Authorities

CHANNELS

Most harbours use VHF and are allocated one or two of the nominated Port Operations channels. These are typically channels 11, 12, 13 or 14 and they can only be used for messages concerning port operations, the movement of ships and, in an emergency, the safety of persons. *Reeds Nautical Almanac, ALRS Small Craft*, or the *Admiralty List of Radio Signals Vol 6* will give details of the working channels of individual harbours.

Port Operation channels

Working channel	Single frequency
11	✔
12	✔
13	✔
14	✔
69	✔
87	✔
88	✔

Services they offer

An increasing number of ports are implementing Vessel Traffic Services (VTS) schemes. These are like a two-dimensional air traffic control and are there to improve efficiency, safety and the protection of the environment. VTS schemes are aimed primarily at commercial vessels, which must comply with the laid down procedures. Small craft operators must check *Reeds Almanac* or pilot books to see whether they too may be affected. For example, Dover Port Control requires all vessels, large and small to seek permission to either enter or leave the harbour.

In busy harbours and restricted visibility, small craft can gain valuable information about the whereabouts of large vessels by listening on the port's working channel. They also give regular broadcasts concerning navigational information.

An example of a Port Operations broadcast

All ships this is Southampton VTS with the harbour information broadcast for ten hundred.

Navigational information:
Survey work in operation close to the Hook Buoy.
Cable recovery vessel anchored across the entrance to the Beaulieu River.
Outbound the *Queen Elizabeth Two* now clearing the Thorn Channel.
Petro Avon now berthing at Fawley.

Tidal information:
Calshot three point five metres above Chart Datum.

Southampton VTS OUT.

PORT OPERATIONS

> **Along with their navigational broadcasts, they give exact tidal heights above LAT, so you can check your tidal calculations as well.**

HARBOUR AUTHORITIES

Harbour authorities are also classed as port operations and therefore use one of the four designated Port Operations channels. They monitor their working channel and CH16, using the dual watch facility on their radio. You should always call a Harbourmaster on his working channel but, as he will be listening in dual watch, he cannot be sure of the channel you actually called him on. So modify the initial call to include the called channel number.

Example of a call to a Harbourmaster

| 12 |

Chichester Harbourmaster, Chichester Harbourmaster,
This is Rosie, Rosie, on Channel 12.
OVER

MARINA CALLS

Working channel	Single frequency	Dual frequency
80		✔
37	✔	

UK marinas have their own working channel, CH80, which is an inter-national dual frequency channel. The dual frequency aspect of CH80 means that one vessel calling Marina Control cannot hear another vessel calling Marina Control, so thinks that the channel is clear. At peak times the capture effect can cause the Marina Control operator to receive a chaotic jumble of the strongest signals. Always use the lowest power available as this will limit interference to other marinas in the area.

Monitor CH80 for 5-10 seconds before transmitting the initial call. Unless a vessel is passing a long message, 5–10 seconds should give sufficient time for the Marina Control operator to be heard if CH80 is in use.

The usual reason for calling a marina is to book a visitor's berth for the night. By making this call, you ensure that there will be a berth that can accommodate the boat and you will know which side to tie the warps and fenders. If your vessel is wide, long or has a deep draught, it is particularly important to check any entry restrictions with the Marina Control. For example, if you were the skipper of a 40ft trimaran with a beam of 28ft you would need to know the width of a lock in order to avoid becoming an instant monohull. Once you have been given a berth number repeat it back to the Dockmaster to confirm you have understood the message.

Making a marina call

Complete your calling card with the following information:

- Name of the marina.
- Marina's working channel.
- Your vessel's name.
- Your vessel's name in phonetics.
- The reason for your call.
- Details of your vessel – length overall, beam, draught, etc.

An example of a marina call

- Select CH80.
- Switch to low power.
- Listen for 10 seconds. If the channel is clear;
- Press the PTT switch and begin your call:

80

Chichester Marina, Chichester Marina.
This is Andante, Andante.
OVER

> Andante.
> This is Chichester Marina.
> OVER

Chichester Marina.
This is Andante.
We would like a berth for two nights.
We are 14 metres in length
with a draught of 2 metres.
OVER

> Andante.
> This is Chichester Marina.
> Go to B59, BRAVO FIFE NINER.
> Fenders starboard side to.
> OVER

Chichester Marina.
This is Andante.
That is BRAVO FIFE NINER.
Fenders starboard side to.
Thank you
OUT

> Andante.
> This is Chichester Marina.
> OUT

PORT
OPERATIONS

15 • DISTRESS

SIGNAL: MAYDAY

DEFINITION

DISTRESS IS DEFINED AS A SITUATION, WHERE, IN THE OPINION OF THE MASTER, A VESSEL, VEHICLE, AIRCRAFT OR PERSON IS IN GRAVE AND IMMINENT DANGER AND REQUIRES IMMEDIATE ASSISTANCE.

ALERTING BY DSC

A Distress call transmitted on the Digital Selective Calling Controller is known as a Distress Alert. A DSC Distress Alert is transmitted on CH70 and is automatically repeated five times to increase the probability of reception. The first one or two alerts may clash with other traffic already using CH70, so by repeating the alert five times, at least one should be successful. Distress Alerts give immediate and absolute priority of communication to the vessel in distress.

A DSC Distress Alert should as far as possible include the vessel's last known position and the time in UTC when it was valid. The position and time may be included automatically if the GPS is interfaced with the DSC equipment, but if you cannot input data automatically from your GPS the position and time will have to be loaded manually. Position should be updated hourly.

To update your position manually, follow this procedure (Note all sets are slightly different):

1 Press MENU.

2 Scroll until you have OTHER on the screen.

3 Press ENTER.

4 Scroll to POSITION.

5 Press ENTER.

```
POSITION                    ▲▼
PRESS ENTER TO SELECT


                            RX 16
232001457      25W          CHAN
```

6 Enter the current latitude.

7 Use the SCROLL button to change
   from N to S.

8 Enter the current longitude.

```
LAT??    99°99'.99   00.00UTC
          ↑
LONG??  99°99'.99
PRESS ENTER TO CONFIRM
                            RX 16
232001478      25W          CHAN
```

9 Use the SCROLL button to change
   from E to W.

10 Enter time UTC (GMT).

11 Press ENTER to confirm.

If the position is not updated within 23.5 hours the position will
default to a series of 9s.

DISTRESS MENU

Undesignated/undefined

This is the default choice when you select DISTRESS. Choose this when
there is no time to compose an alert.

1 Press the DISTRESS button once
   and release.

2 The screen will show
   DISTRESS UNDESIGNATED.

```
DISTRESS UNDESIGNATED   ▲▼

PRESS DISTRESS BUTTON
TO TRANSMIT
                            RX 16
232001478      25W          CHAN
```

DISTRESS

3 Hold down the DISTRESS button for
   five seconds.

> HOLD DISTRESS BUTTON
> FOR 5 SECONDS TO INITIATE
> DISTRESS CALL
>
> 232001478   25W   RX 16 CHAN

4 The radio will count down from
   five.

5 You can cancel the call anytime
   during those 5 seconds.

> MAYDAY SENT
> USE CHANNEL 16
>
> 232001478   25W   RX 16 CHAN

6 After those 5 seconds the alert is
   sent on CH70.

Designated Distress Alert

If you have time to compose the 'nature of distress':

1 Press the DISTRESS button once.

2 The first screen will show
   DISTRESS UNDESIGNATED.

> DISTRESS UNDESIGNATED ▲▼
>
> PRESS DISTRESS BUTTON
> TO TRANSMIT
>
> 232001478   25W   RX 16 CHAN

3 Press SCROLL to access the
   DESIGNATED DISTRESS list.

4 The distress list offered will consist
   of some or all of the following:
   LISTING
   SINKING
   DISABLED
   ABANDONING
   PIRACY
   MAN OVERBOARD
   FIRE

> DISTRESS: FIRE ▲▼
>
> PRESS DISTRESS BUTTON
> TO TRANSMIT
>
> 232001478   25W   RX 16 CHAN

FLOODING	CAPSIZE
COLLISION	EXPLOSION
GROUNDING	UNDESIGNATED.

5 Choose the most appropriate nature of Distress and hold down the DISTRESS button for 5 seconds. The alert will be transmitted.

> HOLD DISTRESS BUTTON
> FOR 5 SECONDS TO INITIATE
> DISTRESS CALL
>
> RX 16
> 232001478   25W   CHAN

> MAYDAY SENT
> USE CHANNEL 16
>
> RX 16
> 232001478   25W   CHAN

When your DSC Distress Alert is received by the Coastguard station's equipment you will get an immediate acknowledgement. If the Distress Alert goes unacknowledged, the DSC Controller will automatically re-broadcast the Distress Alert at between 3.5 and 4.5-minute intervals. However, you can do this manually AT ANY TIME by pressing CANCEL, recomposing the Distress Alert and pressing the DISTRESS button again for 5 seconds. If you receive full assistance from another vessel, cancel the Distress Alert and inform the Coastguard so that he knows you haven't sunk.

PLEASE WAIT 15 SECONDS FOR A DSC ACKNOWLEDGEMENT BEFORE TRANSMITTING YOUR DISTRESS MESSAGE ON CH16.

The Distress Alert sent by a Class D Controller can only be cancelled by: **a)** Turning off the set. **b)** Acknowledgement by Class A or B equipment. **c)** By Shore Station or the Coastguard.

The Coastguard acknowledgement

When the Coastguard acknowledges your Distress Alert you will see this on your screen.

> SEND MAYDAY ON CH16   ▲▼
> ACK FROM 002320014
>
> RX 16
> 232001478   25W   CHAN

DISTRESS

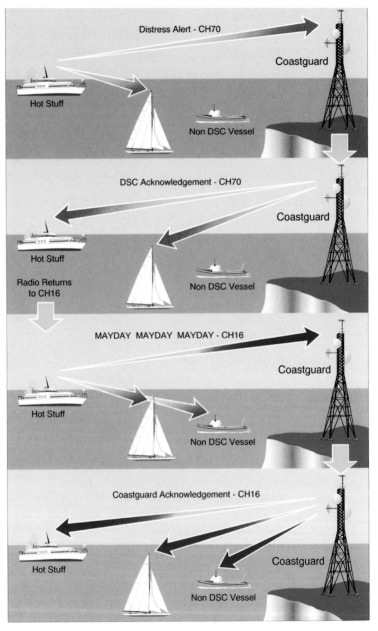

The Distress Alert

THE DISTRESS CALL AND MESSAGE

Once a DSC Distress acknowledgement has been received or after waiting 15 seconds, the vessel in distress should immediately transmit the DISTRESS MESSAGE by voice as follows on Channel 16:

CALL

MAYDAY, MAYDAY, MAYDAY.

This is VESSEL NAME – spoken three times.

MESSAGE

MAYDAY – spoken once.

VESSEL MMSI AND NAME – spoken once.

THE VESSEL'S POSITION preferably using lat/long or a bearing and range from a well-charted object.

The nature of distress.

Assistance required.

Number of persons on board.

Any other information which might help the rescue services.

OVER

DISTRESS

The order of the message ensures that the information is given in the order of importance in case communication is lost. In distress situations, particularly when a vessel is on fire or sinking, the first casualty is often the vessel's battery and with it goes the ship's radio.

To help remember the order of the message, use the mnemonic MIPTAPIO. Each letter will help you to remember a key element of the message (see next page).

Stands for	Detail
M MAYDAY	Spoken once.
I IDENTIFICATION	MMSI number and name of the vessel spoken once.
P POSITION	Expressed as either latitude and longitude OR a bearing and distance FROM a well-charted object. Give the bearing first and range second. It is difficult to determine range accurately by eye so the rescue aircraft will fly to the charted object and follow the bearing until you are sighted.
T TYPE OF DISTRESS	eg on fire, sinking, man overboard on a rough night, etc.
A ASSISTANCE REQUIRED	Immediate assistance required.
P PERSONS ON BOARD	The TOTAL number of persons on board. Don't forget yourself.
I INFORMATION	Information that will help the rescue, eg the frequency of your activated EPIRB; you are abandoning to the liferaft; a description of your vessel; vessel's callsign; you will fire red hand flares at regular intervals and so forth.
O OVER	You want a reply.

If you receive no reply to your Distress Alert on CH70 or Mayday Call and Message broadcast on CH16 re-broadcast your Distress traffic on any other channel you think will obtain a reply.

PROCEDURE CARDS

On a commercial vessel it is a legal requirement for an emergency procedure card to be displayed close to the radio to help anyone transmit a Distress call. Leisure sailors will also find it useful.

Use a procedure card. Below is an example of a procedure card that you can adopt, alter and laminate for your own use. It may help your crew save you.

VHF DISTRESS PROCEDURE

1 TURN RADIO ON, SELECT DISTRESS, PRESS FOR 5 SECONDS.

2 WHEN THE DISTRESS HAS BEEN ACKNOWLEDGED THE RADIO WILL RE-TUNE TO CH16.

3 PASS YOUR CALL AND MESSAGE:

MAYDAY, MAYDAY, MAYDAY

THIS IS HOT STUFF HOT STUFF HOT STUFF

MAYDAY, HOT STUFF 232001478,

MY POSITION IS ... ...

DISTRESS: 'I REQUIRE IMMEDIATE ASSISTANCE'

NUMBER OF PERSONS:

INFORMATION TO AID RESCUE:
EG 30FT MOTORBOAT, BLUE HULL, WHITE DECK.

OVER

CALLSIGN, NAME AND MMSI

M P T Y 9:
MIKE, PAPA, TANGO, YANKEE, NINER.

HOT STUFF:
HOTEL, OSCAR, TANGO – SIERRA, TANGO, UNIFORM, FOXTROT, FOXTROT.

MMSI:
232001478

DISTRESS

An example of a Designated Distress Alert and message.
Note that this will not be the same for all radios.

70

1 Press the DISTRESS button once.

2 The first screen will be DISTRESS
   UNDESIGNATED.

3 Press SCROLL to access the
   Designated Distress list.

4 When you find FIRE press
   DISTRESS BUTTON.

5 Hold down the DISTRESS button
   for 5 seconds and the alert will
   be transmitted.

| DISTRESS: ▲▼ |
| UNDESIGNATED |
| PRESS DISTRESS BUTTON |
| TO TRANSMIT |
| RX 16 |
| 232001478   25W   CHAN |

| DISTRESS: FIRE ▲▼ |
| PRESS DISTRESS BUTTON |
| TO TRANSMIT |
| RX 16 |
| 232001478   25W   CHAN |

| HOLD DISTRESS BUTTON |
| FOR 5 SECONDS TO INITIATE |
| DISTRESS CALL |
| RX 16 |
| 232001478   25W   CHAN |

| MAYDAY SENT |
| USE CHANNEL 16 |
| RX 16 |
| 232001478   25W   CHAN |

16

| CALL | MAYDAY, MAYDAY, MAYDAY.
This is MV HOT STUFF, HOT STUFF, HOT STUFF. |

MESSAGE

M (MAYDAY)	MAYDAY.
I (IDENTITY)	232001478 MV HOT STUFF.
P (POSITION)	49°45'.6N 05°44'.8W.
T (TYPE OF DISTRESS)	On FIRE.
A (ASSISTANCE)	Require immediate assistance.
P (PERSONS)	Five persons on board.
I (INFORMATION)	Abandoning to liferaft. EPIRB activated.
O (OVER)	OVER

DISTRESS

ACKNOWLEDGEMENT OF A DSC DISTRESS ALERT

The International Rules state, 'The obligation to accept Distress calls and messages is absolute in the case of every station without distinction, and such messages must be accepted with priority over all other messages, they must be answered and the necessary steps must immediately be taken to give effect to them.' Although this applies to any vessel, consider the practical implications before leaping into a situation. Coast stations are much better placed to help as they have helicopters, lifeboats, hospitals and other rescue facilities at their disposal. If you acknowledge the receipt of the Distress message, you are implying that you are proceeding to her assistance. The following does not relieve you of your obligation, but it does allow the most practical assistance to be given. Class D sets are unable to send a digital acknowledgement.

When a DSC Controller receives a Distress Alert it will sound an audible alarm. Whilst waiting for the acknowledgement and message:

- Make no transmission.
- Continue the watch on CH16 until the Distress Alert has been acknowledged.
- Plot the casualty's position.
- Write down the message transmitted on CH16.

Depending on the location of the vessel in distress take the following action to acknowledge the alert:

Alert from a vessel within range of the coast: DO NOTHING except listen, plot the casualty's position and tell the skipper. Acknowledgements of a DSC alert by use of DSC is made only by coast stations and vessels fitted with Class A or B DSC Controllers. If there is no response after a short interval, contact the Coastguard and inform them of the Distress situation. When the alert has been acknowledged prepare for receiving the subsequent Distress message. Finally, inform the Master of the vessel of the contents of the Distress message.

Alert from a vessel outside coastal communication range and outside your vicinity: WAIT to see if another vessel, closer to the one in distress, acknowledges the call first. When the alert has been acknowledged prepare for receiving the subsequent Distress message. If no acknowledgement is heard, inform the Master of the vessel of the contents of the Distress message and follow the steps below.

Alert from a vessel out of coastal communication range close-by: ACKNOWLEDGE the Distress as soon as possible. As there is no facility on a Class D Controller to acknowledge a Distress Alert by DSC, it will have to be done on CH16 by voice. Don't panic, take a deep breath and follow this procedure: Transmit the following on CH16:

1 MAYDAY.
2 Name or MMSI number of the vessel in distress spoken 3 times.
3 THIS IS –
4 Name of own vessel spoken 3 times.
5 RECEIVED MAYDAY.
6 State the assistance you can give.

The DSC Distress Alert cycle of five calls will take approximately three seconds and is repeated randomly at between 3.5 and 4.5 minute intervals. If your acknowledgement coincides with a DSC repetition, acknowledge as soon as it is finished.

If you can render full assistance, ask the distressed vessel to cancel the DSC Distress Alert and inform the Coastguard so that he does not assume the vessel has sunk.

Always keep a pencil and notepad by the radio in case you hear a Distress Alert. You will then be able to write down the Distress Message. Remember, you may be the only one to hear it.

DISTRESS ALERT RELAY

A Distress Alert Relay must be sent when a station learns that:

- Another mobile unit is in distress and not in a position to transmit the Distress Alert itself, eg, red flares are sighted.
- The vessel in distress is outside of coast radio range and you have acknowledged his DSC Distress Alert by voice.

A vessel transmitting a Distress Relay message must make it clear that it is not in distress itself. There is no facility on the Class D DSC Controller to send an automatic Distress Relay therefore you must make a DSC Urgency Alert to contact the Coastguard, then transmit a Mayday Relay message by voice on CH16.

Carry out the following procedure:

1 Press MENU.

2 Scroll until you find ALL SHIP SAFETY CALL.

ALL SHIPS CALL ?
PRESS ENTER TO SELECT

RX 16
232001457   25W   CHAN

DISTRESS

3 Press ENTER. This will bring up the
   CALL TO ALL SHIPS screen.

CALL TO ALL SHIPS ?   ▲▼
PRESS ENTER TO SELECT

                           RX 16
232001457   25W   CHAN

4 Press ENTER. This will bring up
   the URGENCY screen.

5 Press ENTER to select.

URGENCY   ▲▼
PRESS ENTER TO SELECT

                           RX 16
232001457   25W   CHAN

6 Press ENTER to send.

7 The radio will re-tune to CH16.

URGENCY   ▲▼
PRESS ENTER TO SEND

                           RX 16
232001457   25W   CHAN

8 The screen will prompt you to
   transmit your URGENCY message.

SEND PAN PAN ON CH 16

                           RX 16
232001457   25W   CHAN

The screen will prompt you to transmit your Urgency message on CH16, which the Controller has selected for you. However, in this instance you are simply grabbing the attention of the Coastguard by using an Urgency Alert while you really intend to transmit a Mayday Relay. I know it is confusing but because of the limitations of the Class D Controller a Mayday Relay can only be done this way. Once you have an acknowledgement by the Coastguard and you are using voice communications, the call must be prefixed Mayday Relay, spoken three times to make it clear that it is not you that is in distress. It takes this form:

MAYDAY RELAY, MAYDAY RELAY, MAYDAY RELAY.

THIS IS: MMSI spoken once and name of your vessel
                        spoken three times.

RECEIVED the
following
MAYDAY from: Name of vessel in distress and MMSI.

BEGINS: Give the message you wrote down or details of
                        the distress.

When a coast station receives a Distress Alert it will relay it as a shore-to-ship Distress Alert Relay to either:

- All ships.
- A selected group of ships.
- A specific ship.

An example of a Mayday Relay call

70

1 Press MENU.

2 Scroll until you find ALL SHIP
  SAFETY CALL.

3 Press ENTER.

4 Press ENTER.

| ALL SHIP SAFETY CALL | ▲▼ |
| PRESS ENTER TO SELECT | |

| | RX 16 |
| 232000763   25W | CHAN |

| CALL TO ALL SHIPS ? | ▲▼ |
| PRESS ENTER TO SELECT | |

| | RX 16 |
| 232000763   25W | CHAN |

DISTRESS

5 Press ENTER.

> URGENCY   ▲▼
> PRESS ENTER TO SELECT
>
>   RX 16
> 232000763   25W   CHAN

6 Press ENTER to send.

> URGENCY   ▲▼
> PRESS ENTER TO SEND
>
>   RX 16
> 232000763   25W   CHAN

7 The radio will re-tune to CH16.

> SEND PAN PAN ON
> CHANNEL 16

8 The screen will prompt you to
   transmit your URGENCY message.

>   RX 16
> 232000763   25W   CHAN

70

MAYDAY RELAY, MAYDAY RELAY, MAYDAY RELAY.
This is 232000763, YACHT ROSIE, ROSIE, ROSIE.

Received the following MAYDAY from MV HOT STUFF 232001478.
MESSAGE BEGINS:
    MAYDAY.
    232001478 MV HOT STUFF.
    TWO ZERO SEVEN degrees from Landsend.
    Lighthouse, twenty miles.
    On fire.
    Require immediate assistance.
    Five persons on board.
    Abandoning to liferaft, EPIRB activated.
    On 121.5 Mhz.
    ENDS
    OVER

CONTROL OF COMMUNICATIONS

When there is Distress working on CH16, silence is automatically imposed. This requires radio communications on CH16 to be controlled and this control is achieved by using a variety of pro-words.

Seelonce Mayday

The station, usually the Coastguard, co-ordinating Distress traffic and any search and rescue operations may impose RADIO SILENCE on other stations that are nothing to do with the distress and which interfere with distress or SAR traffic on CH16. The expression used is SEELONCE MAYDAY and will be used as part of a message broadcast. For example:

MAYDAY.
ALL STATIONS, ALL STATIONS, ALL STATIONS.
This is FALMOUTH COASTGUARD, FALMOUTH COASTGUARD,
FALMOUTH COASTGUARD.
270930 (date and time).
232001478, MV HOT STUFF.
SEELONCE MAYDAY
OUT

Seelonce Distress

Any other station that hears another vessel interfering with the silence may impose silence by using the expression **SEELONCE DISTRESS**. For example:

MAYDAY.
ALL STATIONS, ALL STATIONS, ALL STATIONS.
This is RAINBOW DANCER, RAINBOW DANCER, RAINBOW DANCER.
232001478, MV HOT STUFF.
SEELONCE DISTRESS
OUT

DISTRESS

Prudonce

Distress traffic on CH16 prevents any other traffic being passed and this can be extremely inconvenient when the Distress goes on for a long time. In these situations, once the initial problems have been dealt with but where the Mayday is still ongoing the Coastguard may allow some ESSENTIAL radio traffic to be passed. In this instance he will use the pro-word **PRUDONCE**. It means '**restricted radio working may commence**'. For example:

> MAYDAY.
> ALL STATIONS, ALL STATIONS, ALL STATIONS.
> This is FALMOUTH COASTGUARD, FALMOUTH COASTGUARD,
> FALMOUTH COASTGUARD.
> 271100 (date and time).
> 232001478, MV HOT STUFF.
> **PRUDONCE**
> OUT

Seelonce Fenee

When distress traffic has ceased, the Coastguard controlling the Search and Rescue operations will broadcast a message indicating that Distress is over. On hearing the message normal radio working may re-commence. As it was silence that was imposed it is silence that is lifted. The message you will hear will include the expression **SEELONCE FEENEE**. For example:

> MAYDAY.
> ALL STATIONS, ALL STATIONS, ALL STATIONS.
> This is FALMOUTH COASTGUARD, FALMOUTH COASTGUARD,
> FALMOUTH COASTGUARD.
> 271130 (date and time).
> 232001478, MV HOT STUFF.
> **SEELONCE FEENEE**
> OUT

DIRECTION FINDING

This is an additional type of signal that may be used during Distress working. Lifeboats and some SAR aircraft are fitted with direction finding receivers and may request a vessel in distress to transmit a signal suitable for direction finding. Example:

16

> MAYDAY.
> MV HOT STUFF, MV HOT STUFF, MV HOT STUFF.,
> This is FALMOUTH LIFEBOAT, FALMOUTH LIFEBOAT,
> FALMOUTH LIFEBOAT.
> For D/F purposes will you hold your PTT switch closed for two periods of ten seconds each – followed by your vessel's name repeated four times on this frequency.
> OVER

The reply to this request should be:

> MAYDAY.
> FALMOUTH LIFEBOAT, FALMOUTH LIFEBOAT, FALMOUTH LIFEBOAT.
> This is MV HOT STUFF, MV HOT STUFF, MV HOT STUFF.
> (10 sec PTT – 10 sec PTT) – HOT STUFF, HOT STUFF, HOT STUFF, HOT STUFF.
> OVER

CANCELLING A FALSE ALARM

False Distress Alerts can put a significant burden on the Search and Rescue services. The chance that a false alert will coincide with an actual distress is high and as a consequence Search and Rescue services could be delayed in responding to a real distress.

If you transmit a false Distress Alert:
1 Allow transmission to complete once.
2 Switch off transmitter to stop repetitions.
3 Switch the equipment back on and select CH16.
4 Make a broadcast to All Stations:

DISTRESS

ALL STATIONS, ALL STATIONS, ALL STATIONS.
This is: MMSI and NAME – 3 times.
POSITION:
Cancel my Distress Alert of – date and time UTC.

Once a Distress Alert has been sent the Coastguard will know your
MMSI number and with it all the details he requires to trace you and
your boat. So you must admit your mistake immediately.

**Try to install the radio out of the reach of inquisitive,
bored or rebellious children.**

16 • URGENCY

SIGNAL: PAN PAN

DEFINITION

The Urgency Signal Pan Pan indicates that the station sending it has a very urgent message to transmit concerning the safety of a ship, aircraft, vehicle or person. It is used where there is no **imminent** danger to a ship or person and **immediate** assistance is NOT required or fully justified. The signal has priority over all other communications except distress and can only be sent with the permission of the Master of the vessel.

It is sometimes difficult to decide whether a situation is grave and imminent or simply urgent and only the person responsible for the vessel can decide this. An Urgency situation after time may need to be upgraded to a Mayday.

The rescue services prefer to be called whilst you are in open water and, if possible whilst there is still daylight. One hour of daylight is worth eight hours of darkness.

ALERTING BY DSC

One big difference between a DSC Distress Alert and an Urgency Alert is that position is not automatically included in the Urgency Alert. I know you are saying to yourselves 'When I've paid all this money for a radio that shows position automatically, why is it not sent automatically in the Urgency call?' The only answer I have been given to that question is that some wacky bit of the Radio Regulations does not allow it – yet!

1 Press MENU.

2 Scroll until you find ALL SHIP CALL.

```
ALL SHIP CALL                    ▲▼
PRESS ENTER TO SELECT


                                 RX 16
232001457        25W             CHAN
```

3 Press ENTER. This will bring up the CALL TO ALL SHIPS screen.

```
CALL TO ALL SHIPS ?              ▲▼
PRESS ENTER TO SELECT


                                 RX 16
232001457        25W             CHAN
```

4 Press ENTER. This will bring up the URGENCY screen.

```
URGENCY                          ▲▼
PRESS ENTER TO SELECT


                                 RX 16
232001457        25W             CHAN
```

5 Press ENTER to select.

6 Press ENTER to send.

```
URGENCY                          ▲▼
PRESS ENTER TO SELECT


                                 RX 16
232001457        25W             CHAN
```

7 The radio will re-tune to CH16.

8 The screen will prompt you to transmit your URGENCY message.

```
SEND PAN PAN ON
CHANNEL 16


                                 RX 16
232001457        25W             CHAN
```

PAN PAN MESSAGE

It is addressed to 'all stations' or an individual Coastguard station. The transmission of an Urgency message is as follows:

PAN PAN – PAN PAN – PAN PAN
ALL STATIONS or individual Coastguard station – spoken
three times.
THIS IS:
MMSI number and the name, or callsign of own vessel – spoken
three times.

From this point on the order of the message is PRANIO:

P **POSITION**   Either Lat/long or a bearing and range
                             from a well-charted object.

R **REASON FOR CALL**
A **ASSISTANCE REQUIRED**
N **NUMBER ON BOARD**
I **INFORMATION TO HELP RESCUE**
O **OVER**

An example of a PAN PAN call

70

1 Press MENU.

2 Scroll until you find ALL SHIP
   SAFETY CALL.

3 Press ENTER. This will bring up the
   CALL TO ALL SHIPS screen.

4 Press ENTER. This will bring up the
   URGENCY screen.

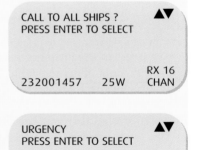

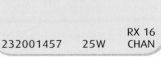

URGENCY

5 Press ENTER to select.

6 Press ENTER to send.

> URGENCY   ▲▼
> PRESS ENTER TO SEND
>
>   RX 16
> 232001457   25W   CHAN

7 The radio will re-tune to CH16 .

8 The screen will prompt you to transmit your PAN PAN message.

> SEND PAN PAN ON
> CHANNEL 16
>
>   RX 16
> 232001457   25W   CHAN

16 | PAN PAN, PAN PAN, PAN PAN
ALL STATIONS, ALL STATIONS, ALL STATIONS.
This is 232001468 BOSUN'S DREAM.
My position is 50°37'.9 N 000° 54'.6 W.
Engine failure.
Require a tow.
Four persons on board.
Drifting rapidly towards the shore.
OVER

URGENT MEDICAL ADVICE

If you have an urgent message about the health of a person, but the condition is not life-threatening; you can be put in touch with a doctor ashore for medical advice. Make the call in the same way you would a Pan Pan call. Once the call has been acknowledged pass the message on CH16 stating that you need **Urgent Medical Advice.**

The Coastguard will co-ordinate the medical assistance by telephoning a doctor from a nominated hospital and the doctor will be linked to the vessel via an appropriate VHF working channel. You will be asked to re-tune your radio to the allocated working channel and the doctor will speak to you as soon as the link can be established. This call is free. The Coastguard will monitor the call in case a helicopter or lifeboat is required.

Please remember to have details of the casualty and his symptoms to hand.

 Before setting sail, ask all crew members for details of any medical condition they may have or special drugs they require and ensure that they have brought along a supply. Keep a note of the contents of the ship's first aid kit and medicine chest by the radio so that valuable time is not wasted when summoning help or advice.

RECEPTION OF AN URGENCY MESSAGE

Vessels receiving a DSC Urgency call announcing an Urgency message addressed to 'All Ships' must listen to the Urgency message on CH16 and assess whether they are able to offer assistance.

URGENCY

17 • THE SAFETY CALL

SIGNAL: SECURITE

DEFINITION

The Safety signal 'Securite' indicates that the calling station has as important navigational or meteorological warning to transmit. Most Safety messages originate from coast stations.

ALERTING BY COAST STATIONS

The announcement of a Safety message by a coast station is made on CH70 by DSC and on CH16. This call simply alerts you to the working channel on which the Safety message will be passed. If you receive it on DSC, press ENTER and the radio will automatically change to the working channel selected. If you hear it on CH16, you will have to manually re-tune the radio if the message is to be passed on a working channel. The DSC Alert sound is only used for new gale warnings and urgent navigational warnings not routine information.

Example of a shore to ship Securite call

SECURITE, SECURITE, SECURITE.
ALL STATIONS, ALL STATIONS, ALL STATIONS.
This is SOLENT COASTGUARD, SOLENT COASTGUARD,
SOLENT COASTGUARD.
For the latest weather bulletin and navigational warnings
listen on CH73.

Passing a Safety message to the Coastguard

If you sight a navigation buoy adrift and you are within radio range of the coast, call the nearest Coastguard station and allow them to re-broadcast the Safety message using their more powerful transmitter. To call the Coastguard follow this procedure:

70
1 Press MENU on the DSC Controller.

2 Scroll to INDIVIDUAL CALL.

3 Press ENTER.

4 Press MANUAL to enter MMSI or DIRECTORY if MMSI stored.

MANUAL MMS1? [002320011]

5 Press ENTER to select.

6 Enter the MMSI of the Coastguard (Solent CG is 002320011).

RX 16
232001457   25W   CHAN

7 Press ENTER to confirm.

8 Press ENTER to send call.

The radio will automatically re-tune to CH16 or a working channel as required in the acknowledgement sent by the CG so that the message can be passed to the Coastguard by voice as follows:

16
Solent Coastguard, Solent Coastguard, Solent Coastguard.
This is 232001457.
Rainbow Dancer, Rainbow Dancer, Rainbow Dancer.
I have safety traffic for you.
OVER

> Rainbow Dancer.
> This is Solent Coastguard.
> Go ahead please.
> OVER

Solent Coastguard.
This is Rainbow Dancer.
My position is 185°(T) St. Catherine's Lighthouse 4.25 nm.
I have sighted a starboard hand navigation buoy drifting West.
Approximately half a mile due North of my position.
OVER

THE SAFETY CALL

ALERTING BY INDIVIDUAL VESSELS TO 'ALL SHIPS'

If your engine has broken down and you are adrift in the shipping lanes outside coastal radio range, you pose a safety risk to other vessels as well as yourself. In this instance you would want to warn other vessels of your position and this can be done by transmitting an ALL SHIPS SAFETY CALL by DSC on CH70. To do this follow this procedure:

1 Press MENU.

2 Scroll until you find ALL SHIP SAFETY CALL.

3 Press ENTER. This will bring up the CALL TO ALL SHIPS screen.

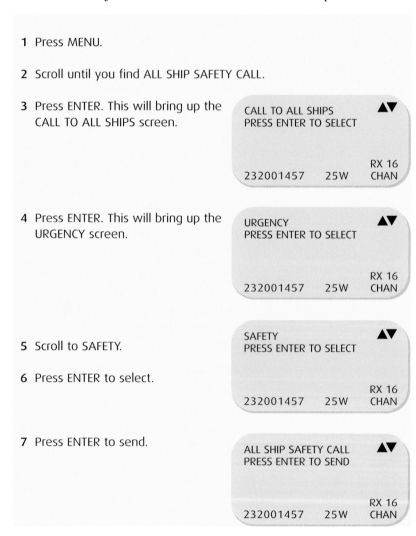

CALL TO ALL SHIPS
PRESS ENTER TO SELECT

RX 16
232001457   25W   CHAN

4 Press ENTER. This will bring up the URGENCY screen.

URGENCY
PRESS ENTER TO SELECT

RX 16
232001457   25W   CHAN

5 Scroll to SAFETY.

6 Press ENTER to select.

SAFETY
PRESS ENTER TO SELECT

RX 16
232001457   25W   CHAN

7 Press ENTER to send.

ALL SHIP SAFETY CALL
PRESS ENTER TO SEND

RX 16
232001457   25W   CHAN

8 The radio will re-tune to a working channel.

9 The screen will prompt you to transmit your SAFETY message.

> SEND SAFETY MESSAGE ON CHANNEL 16
>
> 232001457   25W   RX 16 CHAN

Safety message by individual vessel to 'All Ships'

Once you are re-tuned to CH16 you need to transmit the Safety message as follows:

SECURITE, SECURITE, SECURITE.
ALL STATIONS or called station – spoken three times.
THIS IS:
The MMSI and name or callsign of own vessel – spoken three times.
The text of the Safety message.

Example of an All Ships Safety message

SECURITE, SECURITE, SECURITE.
ALL SHIPS, ALL SHIPS, ALL SHIPS.
This is 232001458.
MACH TWO.
My engines are broken down and I am drifting.
My position is: fifty degrees zero eight decimal two North,
zero degrees fifty eight decimal four West.
I request you give me a wide berth.
OUT

RECEPTION OF A SAFETY MESSAGE

Vessels receiving a DSC Safety Call announcing a Safety message addressed to 'All Ships' should allow the radio to re-tune to the channel selected and then monitor it for the message.

THE SAFETY CALL

18 • MOBILE PHONES VERSUS VHF RADIO

It is often suggested that a mobile phone is an effective alternative to a marine VHF radio. It is true that there is now good coverage of coastal waters and indeed the coverage in some areas is better than VHF, which only has a radio horizon of 30-40 miles from the coast. It is also true that they are cost effective for making phone calls – hence the demise of the Coast Radio Stations that once handled phone calls via the VHF radio system. Although you can make a 999 emergency call and ask for the Coastguard, the call will not necessarily be routed to the nearest Coastguard. As the cellular systems are national, with only one or two operators for the entire UK, your call could end up at a Coastguard Rescue Co-ordination Centre anywhere around the UK coast.

Mobile phones do provide the convenience of a simple, easy-to-use, inexpensive, private and generally reliable telephone service to home, office, car or other location providing you are within range of an antenna on the coast. Mobile phone receiving antennas are designed for maximum land coverage so are tuned toward land, not the sea and in some places there is no mobile phone coverage at all.

Conversely, VHF marine radios are designed and recommended for use with safety at sea in mind. When in distress, calls can be received not only by the Coastguard but also by ships that may be in a position to give immediate assistance. A VHF marine radio also helps ensure that weather warnings and other urgent navigational information broadcasts are received. The Coastguard announces these broadcasts on DSC CH70 and VHF CH16 and timely receipt of such information may save your life. Additionally, your VHF marine radio can be used in other countries, whereas your mobile phone may be restricted in its use.

MOBILE PHONES ON BOATS

The safety organisations do not advocate mobile phones as a substitute for the regular VHF marine radio systems except to chat to friends or personnel on other boats. Nevertheless mobile phones can have a place on board as an additional safety measure.

Why a mobile phone is limited in an emergency

- Mobile phone calls are not free of charge, although HMCG is the fourth emergency service and a 999 call is free. If you call a Coastguard station on their direct number you will incur charges and if you use a pre-paid service your phone may run short of funds and disconnect.
- Mobile phones are not waterproof or designed for the rough and corrosive marine environment. Try taking yours in the shower with you and see what happens!
- Mobile phones generally cannot provide ship to ship safety communications, neither can you talk directly to rescue craft trying to find you unless they also have a cell phone. For this you need a marine VHF radio.
- If you make a distress call on a mobile phone, only the person you call will be able to hear you.
- Your call will not have the priority access given to a VHF distress call.
- Most mobile phones are designed for use on land so their coverage offshore may be limited and change without notice.
- Mobile phone antennas are rarely placed on the coast so if you're beneath a steep cliff your signal is unlikely to be detected.
- Locating a mobile caller in trouble without a precise position is hard to do as the Coastguard direction finding equipment does not detect on mobile phone frequencies.
- Calling your Dad to raise the alarm is not a good idea either, as messages are likely to become muddled. 'Pooped off Looe' offers all kinds of opportunities for a non-sailor.

Should you rely exclusively on a mobile phone?

No, a mobile phone is not equivalent to a VHF marine radio. Each provides a different service. The mobile phone is best used for what it is: a link with shore based telephones. A VHF marine radio is intended for communication with other ships, rescue aircraft and other marine installations.

Clearly, there are no objections to taking a mobile telephone aboard but if you are boating offshore, a mobile phone is no substitute for a

MOBILE PHONE
VERSUS VHF RADIO

VHF radio. If you are within mobile range, it may provide an additional means of communication to your marine VHF radio and if you need to use your mobile phone to report an incident at sea, the following guidelines should be used:

DO

1 Use an external aerial.

2 Provide the emergency services with:
   - your mobile phone number so that you can be contacted.
   - name and any other identification of the vessel in trouble
   - position
   - description of the problem
   - number of people on board
   - brief description of the vessel
   - any other relevant information.

3 Once you have reported the emergency, keep the line free for contact by the Search and Rescue services.

4 Conserve battery power as much as possible.

5 Ensure you have topped-up funds if you use a pre-paid service.

6 Try to keep the phone dry.

DON'T

1 Don't use a mobile phone instead of a proper marine VHF radio.

2 Don't hang up after talking to Search and Rescue services unless you both agree to do so.

3 Don't make any other phone calls until the rescue services have finished their job.

19 • OTHER –
HOUSEKEEPING FUNCTIONS

No, although the title suggests it, you won't need to don an apron and rubber gloves for this. 'Housekeeping' is the term given to the support functions of the DSC Controller and is dealt with under OTHER in the CALL menu.

These functions are:

- To store an MMSI in the directory.
- To enter a manual position and time.
- To enter a group MMSI number.
- The self-test facility. The self-test facility tests the internal functions of the radio and does not transmit a signal. It is not a feature on all radios. To test the transmitted signal, arrange to call another vessel by DSC.

OTHER

1 Press MENU.

2 Use the SCROLL button until you find OTHER.

3 Press ENTER.

```
OTHER                    ▲▼
PRESS ENTER TO SELECT



                              RX 16
232001457      1W       CHAN
```

For each individual function, follow these procedures:

Storing an MMSI in the directory

1 Press MENU.

2 Scroll until you have OTHER on
   the screen.

3 Press ENTER.

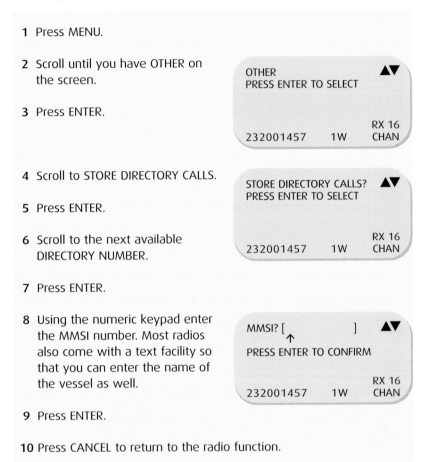

4 Scroll to STORE DIRECTORY CALLS.

5 Press ENTER.

6 Scroll to the next available
   DIRECTORY NUMBER.

7 Press ENTER.

8 Using the numeric keypad enter
   the MMSI number. Most radios
   also come with a text facility so
   that you can enter the name of
   the vessel as well.

9 Press ENTER.

10 Press CANCEL to return to the radio function.

Enter a manual position

If you cannot input data automatically from your GPS, the position
and time will have to be loaded manually through the numeric keypad
and ENTER button.

It is important to develop a system whereby the position and time is updated regularly. It is recommended that you do this hourly, when you update your ship's log, if not, at least every four hours.

To update your position manually, follow this procedure:

1 Press MENU.

2 Scroll until you have OTHER on the screen.

3 Press ENTER.

```
OTHER                         ▲▼
PRESS ENTER TO SELECT


                              RX 16
232001457      1W             CHAN
```

4 Scroll to POSITION.

5 Press ENTER.

```
ENTER POSITION                ▲▼
PRESS ENTER TO SELECT


                              RX 16
232001457      1W             CHAN
```

6 Enter current latitude position using the numeric keypad.

7 Use the SCROLL button to change from N to S.

```
LAT?      99°99'.99   00.00 UTC
           ↑
LONG?     99°99'.99           ▲▼
PRESS ENTER TO CONFIRM
                              RX 16
232001478      1W             CHAN
```

8 Enter current longitude.

9 Use the SCROLL button to change from E to W.

10 Enter time UTC (GMT).

11 Press ENTER to confirm

12 If the position is not updated within 23.5 hours the position will default to a series of 9s.

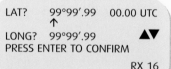
OTHER –
HOUSEKEEPING

To enter a Group MMSI

Flotillas, races and clubs can use a Group MMSI for the day. The number is decided by the group and any number can be used provided it does not start with 00 which would imply that you are a coast station. To prevent this, the first digit (0) will be included automatically by the DSC Controller but any attempt to use 0 as the second digit will be rejected. Each member of the particular group will enter the number into the DSC Controller under the OTHER menu. Their radios will respond to both their individual MMSI and the Group MMSI. Now enter the number in the Directory so that it is ready for use. A Group MMSI cannot be used as a vessel's identity. Some radios may differ slightly so check the manual.

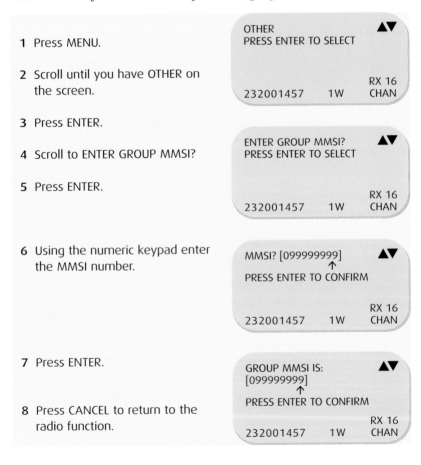

1 Press MENU.

    OTHER   ▲▼
    PRESS ENTER TO SELECT

2 Scroll until you have OTHER on
   the screen.
                                                          RX 16
    232001457   1W   CHAN

3 Press ENTER.

4 Scroll to ENTER GROUP MMSI?

    ENTER GROUP MMSI?   ▲▼
    PRESS ENTER TO SELECT

5 Press ENTER.
                                                          RX 16
    232001457   1W   CHAN

6 Using the numeric keypad enter
   the MMSI number.

    MMSI? [099999999]   ▲▼
                      ↑
    PRESS ENTER TO CONFIRM

                                                          RX 16
    232001457   1W   CHAN

7 Press ENTER.

    GROUP MMSI IS: ▲▼
    [099999999]
                  ↑
    PRESS ENTER TO CONFIRM

8 Press CANCEL to return to the
   radio function.
                                                          RX 16
    232001457   1W   CHAN

Self-test

(Not available on some sets)

1 Press MENU.

2 Scroll until you have OTHER on the screen.

3 Press ENTER.

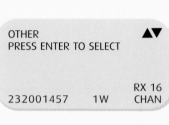

4 Scroll to SELF TEST.

5 Press ENTER.

6 Each function tested will appear on the screen.

7 An alarm will sound and SELF-TEST COMPLETED will appear unless there is a fault to report.

8 Press CANCEL to return to the radio function.

OTHER   ▲▼
PRESS ENTER TO SELECT

                                   RX 16
232001457   1W   CHAN

SELF-TEST   ▲▼
PRESS ENTER TO SELECT

                                   RX 16
232001457   1W   CHAN

TESTING MEMORY

                                   RX 16
232001457   1W   CHAN

SELF-TEST COMPLETED

                                   RX 16
232001457   1W   CHAN

OTHER –
HOUSEKEEPING

QUIZ 2 • 40 QUESTIONS

1 Spell RADIOTELEPHONE using the phonetic alphabet.

2 What does the pro-word OVER signify?

3 What does the pro-word OUT signify?

4 Is it permissible to say OVER AND OUT at the end of a message?

5 If you want all or part of a message repeating, what pro-words would you use?

6 Is it permissible to make a transmission without identification?

7 Is it permissible to call a ship by her name rather than her call-sign or MMSI number in normal voice transmissions?

8 Is it permissible to use a person's name instead of the vessel's name or callsign?

9 If you hear a call but are unsure that the call was for you, what action should you take?

10 If a call goes unanswered, how long must you wait before trying again.

11 When calling a Coast Station, who controls the call?

12 What are the four exclusive intership channels?

13 What is the primary intership channel that must be fitted to all VHF radios?

14 What channel would you use in confined waters to call a ship to discuss collision avoidance?

15 Is it permitted to call another vessel direct on an intership channel?

16 What does the MANUAL option on your DSC Controller allow you to do?

17 What does the DIRECTORY option on your DSC Controller allow you to do?

18 How often is the routine weather forecast broadcast by the Coastguard?

QUIZ 2 • 40 QUESTIONS

19 What channel(s) do the Coastguard use for the initial announcement of navigational warnings and weather forecasts?

20 When calling a Harbour Authority do you make the initial call on CH16 or their working channel?

21 Where can you find details of the working channels of individual ports or harbours?

22 During Distress working, when the Controlling Station wishes to indicate that restricted radio working may commence on CH16, what pro-words does he use?

23 At the end of Distress working, when the Controlling Station wishes to indicate that the Mayday is over, what pro-words are used?

24 Under what circumstances would you transmit a Distress Alert?

25 How many consecutive Distress Alerts are transmitted by the DSC Controller at one time?

26 When transmitting an Undesignated Distress Alert, what three pieces of information are included in the alert?

27 Is it possible to cancel the Distress Alert during the 5-second countdown?

28 When passing on someone else's Distress, what call is used to signify that it is not your vessel that is in trouble?

29 During Distress working, when the Controlling Station wishes to impose radio silence on vessels using CH16 for non Distress traffic, what pro-words does he use?

30 Your motor vessel's name is COOL IT, callsign MGTH7, MMSI 232001928. You are on fire and the fire is out of control. You and your three other crew are about to abandon to the liferaft. You are about to set off your 121.5MHz EPIRB. It is 0900 hours UTC and you have not updated your position in your DSC Controller for 10 hours. From your present position you are five miles off of St Catherine's Lighthouse which bears 305°(T). Write down the actions you will take to send the call and write down

QUIZ 2 • 40 QUESTIONS

a) the type of call you will send.
b) the channel(s) on which you will send the call and message.
c) the mode (DSC or voice) of each part.
d) the details contained in each part.

31 Your yacht's name is SEALEGS, callsign MRUS6, MMSI 232002819. It is 1800 hours and you are sinking rapidly. You and your four other crew are about to abandon to the liferaft. You are about to set off your 406MHz EPIRB. Your GPS position is 50° 38'.2 N 000° 49'.3 W. Write down the actions you will take to send the call and write down the wording of the message. Indicate:
a) the type of call you will send.
b) the channel(s) on which you will send the call and message.
c) the mode (DSC or voice) of each part.
d) the details contained in each part.

32 Your yacht's name is JOLLY ROGER, callsign GTSH, MMSI 232001829. Your sails have blown out, your engine will not start and you are being blown onto a lee shore. You have one other crew and two children on board. You are about to set off your 121.5MHz EPIRB and have six red handflares available. You have no position in your DSC Controller. You are two miles East of St Anthony's Light. Write down the actions you will take to send the call and write down the wording of the message. Indicate:
a) the type of call you will send.
b) the channel(s) on which you will send the call and message.
c) the mode (DSC or voice) of each part.
d) the details contained in each part.

33 What does the Urgency call indicate?

34 What word is used to signify an Urgency call?

35 If you want medical advice what DSC call would you use?

36 Your vessel FULL BORE is a 38ft motorboat and the MMSI is 232007085. You have not updated your position in the DSC Controller. Your engine has broken down and you require a tow. You have three other crew on board. From your present position St Catherine's Lighthouse bears 205°(T), range approximately

QUIZ 2 • 40 QUESTIONS

six miles. Write down the actions you will take to send the call and write down the wording of the message. Indicate:

a) the type of call you will send.
b) the channel(s) on which you will send the call and message.
c) the mode (DSC or voice) of each part.
d) the details contained in each part.

37 Your vessel is a 28ft sailing boat with a red hull and teak decks. Its name is KIWI, the MMSI is 232007086 and its callsign is MSYE8. Your rudder has broken off and you require a tow. You have two other crew on board. From your GPS your present position is 50° 32'.2 N 001° 19'.3 W. Write down the actions you will take to send the call and write down the wording of the message. Indicate:

a) the type of call you will send.
b) the channel(s) on which you will send the call and message.
c) the mode (DSC or voice) of each part.
d) the details contained in each part.

38 One of your crew is suffering from extreme abdominal pain and you want some medical advice. Your vessel is a 38ft ketch-rigged yacht with a white hull and blue deck. Its name is OYSTER the MMSI is 232007056 and its callsign is MLAU2. From your GPS your present position is 50° 28'.2 N 001° 29'.3 W. Write down the actions you will take to send the call and write down the wording of the message. Indicate:

a) the type of call you will send.
b) the channel(s) on which you will send the call and message.
c) the mode (DSC or voice) of each part.
d) the details contained in each part.

39 What signal words indicate that a navigational or meteorological warning follows?

40 If you are within range of a Coastguard station and you sight a floating mine, would you transmit an 'All Ships Safety Call' by DSC, or call the Coastguard by DSC?

Answers on pages 124–128.

QUIZ 2 • ANSWERS

1 Romeo, Alpha, Delta, India, Oscar, Tango, Echo, Lima, Echo, Papa, Hotel, Oscar, November, Echo.

2 A reply is expected.

3 No reply is expected.

4 No.

5 Say Again.

6 No.

7 Yes.

8 No.

9 Do nothing. Wait for the call to be repeated.

10 Two minutes.

11 The Coast Station.

12 6, 8, 72, 77.

13 CH06.

14 CH13.

15 Yes.

16 It allows you to input an MMSI into your DSC Controller.

17 It allows you to store a number of MMSI numbers for quick reference.

18 Every four hours.

19 CH70 and CH16.

20 Working channel.

21 *Reeds Nautical Almanac* or the *Admiralty List of Radio Signals Volume 6*.

22 Prudonce.

23 Seelonce Feenee.

QUIZ 2 • ANSWERS

24 When a vessel, vehicle, aircraft or person is in grave and imminent danger and requires immediate assistance.

25 Five.

26 MMSI, position and time the position was valid.

27 Yes.

28 Mayday Relay.

29 Seelonce Mayday.

30 a) Distress.
   b) Alert – CH70. Message – CH16.
   c) CH70 – DSC. CH16 – voice.
   d) **Details contained in Distress Alert:**
      232001928.
      Position as at 2300 hours UTC.
      Designated distress – Fire.
      Details contained in Distress Message:
      Mayday, Mayday, Mayday.
      This is MV Cool It, Cool It, Cool It.
      Mayday.
      232001928, MV Cool It.
      125°(T) St Catherine's Lighthouse, 5 miles.
      On fire, fire is out of control.
      Require immediate assistance.
      4 persons on board.
      Abandoning to liferaft. EPIRB activated on 121.5MHz.
      Callsign MGTH7.
      OVER.

31 a) Distress.
   b) Alert – CH70. Message – CH16
   c) CH70 – DSC. CH16 – voice.
   d) **Details contained in Distress Alert:**
      232002819.
      50° 38'.2 N 000° 49'.3W, 1800 hours UTC.
      Designated Distress – Sinking.

QUIZ 2 • ANSWERS

Details contained in Distress Message:
Mayday, Mayday, Mayday.
This is Yacht Sealegs, Sealegs, Sealegs.
Mayday.
232002819, Yacht Sealegs.
50° 38'.2 N 000° 49'.3W.
Sinking rapidly.
Require immediate assistance.
5 persons on board.
Abandoning to liferaft. EPIRB activated on 406MHz.
Callsign MRUS6.
OVER.

32 a) Distress.
b) Alert – CH70. Message – CH16.
c) CH70 – DSC. CH16 – voice.
d) Details contained in Distress Alert:
232001829
No position sent.
Designated Distress – Disabled
Details contained in Distress Message:
Mayday, Mayday, Mayday.
This is Yacht Jolly Roger, Jolly Roger, Jolly Roger.
Mayday.
232001829, Yacht Jolly Roger.
090°(T) St Anthony's Light, 2 miles.
Sails blown out, engine won't start, being blown onto lee shore.
Require immediate assistance.
4 persons on board.
Abandoning to liferaft. EPIRB activated on 121.5MHz.
Callsign GTSH.
OVER.

33 The Urgency signal indicates that the station sending it has a very urgent message to transmit concerning the safety of a vessel, vehicle, aircraft or person. There is no imminent danger and immediate assistance is not fully justified.

QUIZ 2 • ANSWERS

34 Pan Pan.

35 Urgency.

36 a) Urgency.
   b) Alert – CH70. Message – CH16.
   c) CH70 – DSC. CH16 – voice.
   d) **Details contained in Urgency Alert:**
      232007085.
      Urgency.
      Details contained in Urgency Message:
      Pan Pan, Pan Pan, Pan Pan.
      All Stations, All Stations, All Stations,
      This is 232007085 M.V. Full Bore, Full Bore, Full Bore.
      My position is 025°(T) St Catherine's Lighthouse, 6 miles.
      Engine broken down.
      Require a tow.
      4 persons on board.
      OVER.

37 a) Urgency.
   b) Alert – CH70. Message – CH16.
   c) CH70 – DSC. CH16 – voice.
   d) **Details contained in Urgency Alert:**
      232007086.
      Urgency.
      Details contained in Urgency Message:
      Pan Pan, Pan Pan, Pan Pan.
      All Stations, All Stations, All Stations.
      This is 232007086 Yacht Kiwi, Kiwi, Kiwi.
      My position is 50° 32.2 N 001° 19.3W.
      The rudder has broken off.
      Require a tow.
      3 persons on board.
      The vessel is a 28ft sailing boat with a red hull and teak
      decks, callsign MSYE8.
      OVER.

QUIZ 2 • ANSWERS

38 a) Urgency.
   b) Alert – CH70. Message – CH16.
   c) CH70 - DSC. CH16 - voice.
   d) **Details contained in Urgency Alert:**
      232007056.
      Urgency.
      Details contained in Urgency Message:
      Pan Pan, Pan Pan, Pan Pan.
      All Stations, All Stations, All Stations.
      This is 232007056 Yacht Oyster.
      My position is 50° 28'.2 N 001° 29'.3W.
      I require Urgent Medical Advice, callsign MLAU2.
      OVER.

39 Securite, Securite, Securite.

40 Call by DSC to Coastguard.

Quick Call Guide

Distress/Mayday ● ***Mayday Relay*** ● ***Urgency***
Safety ● ***Routine*** ● ***Calling a marina***

DISTRESS

DSC – Undesignated

With no time to compose the Distress call, send an Undesignated Alert:

70

1 Lift the flap and press the DISTRESS button once and release.
2 The screen (if available) will show DISTRESS UNDESIGNATED.
3 Hold down the DISTRESS BUTTON for five seconds. The radio will count down from five.
4 You can cancel the call any time during the 5 second countdown.
5 After 5 seconds has elapsed the Alert is sent on CH70.

DSC – Designated

With time to compose the Distress Alert send a Designated Alert:

70

1 Lift the flap and press the DISTRESS button once and release.
2 The screen (if available) will show DISTRESS UNDESIGNATED.
3 Scroll to find the appropriate nature of distress.
4 Hold down the DISTRESS button for five seconds. The radio will count down from five.
5 The call can be CANCELLED at any time during the 5 second count-down.
6 After 5 seconds has elapsed the alert is sent on CH70.

Channel 16 voice call and message

Once acknowledged the radio will re-tune to CH16 where you will transmit the following:

16

MAYDAY, MAYDAY, MAYDAY.
THIS IS:
VESSEL NAME spoken three times and MMSI (DSC only) or callsign spoken once.

MAYDAY – spoken once.
VESSEL NAME AND MMSI – spoken once.
The vessel's POSITION, by latitude and longitude or distance FROM a well known landmark.
Whether in liferaft?
The nature of DISTRESS (sinking, fire etc).
Type of ASSISTANCE desired.
Number of PEOPLE on board.
Any other INFORMATION which might help the rescue services such as hull colour, EPIRB.
OVER

MAYDAY RELAY

Using DSC

There is no facility on the Class D DSC Controller to send an automatic Distress Relay because one distressed vessel can generate hundreds of Distress Relay Alerts. Recreational craft must make a DSC Urgency Alert to contact the Coastguard, then transmit a Mayday Relay message by voice on CH16.

To make the DSC Alert and call:

70

1 Select ALL SHIPS then URGENCY from the DSC menu.
2 Press ENTER to send.
3 The radio will re-tune to CH16.
4 The screen will prompt you to transmit your message.

Voice

Apart from the DSC front end, a Mayday Relay on a non-DSC radio is the same as the CH16 part of the DSC procedure. Transmit the call prefixed by MAYDAY RELAY.

This is what to say:

16

MAYDAY RELAY, MAYDAY RELAY, MAYDAY RELAY.
THIS IS MMSI spoken once (DSC only) and name of your vessel spoken three times.
RECEIVED THE FOLLOWING MAYDAY FROM (Name of vessel in distress and MMSI).
MESSAGE BEGINS:
Transmit the message you wrote down or details of the distress.
OVER

URGENCY

DSC

To make the DSC alert and call:

70

1 Select from the DSC menu ALL SHIPS then URGENCY.
2 Press ENTER to send.
3 The radio will re-tune to CH16.
4 The screen will prompt you to transmit your (PAN PAN) message.

Pan Pan call and message for DSC and non-DSC radios

This call is addressed to All Stations or an individual Coastguard
station. A guide to the format is as follows:

16

PAN PAN – PAN PAN – PAN PAN.
ALL STATIONS or individual Coastguard station – spoken three times
THIS IS:
MMSI and NAME, or CALLSIGN of own vessel – spoken three times.
POSITION, either latitude and longitude co-ordinates or range and
bearing from a land mark.
DETAILS of URGENT situation.
Over

SAFETY

Calling the Coastguard – DSC

70

Select INDIVIDUAL CALL from the DSC menu.
Either manually enter MMSI or select from the DIRECTORY.
Press ENTER to send alert.

The radio will automatically re-tune to the selected working channel for the message to be passed by voice as follows:

WORKING
CHANNEL

NAME OF COASTGUARD.
THIS IS – MMSI and NAME.
REASON for call.
OVER

Calling the Coastguard – voice

16

NAME OF COASTGUARD – three times.
THIS IS – three times.
OVER

Listen for the working channel in the Coastguard reply. Tune to the working channel and pass your message.

All Ships Safety Call – DSC

70

Select ALL SHIP SAFETY CALL from the menu.
Select SAFETY.
Press ENTER to send.
The radio will re-tune to CH16.
The screen will prompt you to transmit your SAFETY MESSAGE.

WORKING CHANNEL	SECURITE, SECURITE, SECURITE. ALL STATIONS or called station – spoken three times. THIS IS – MMSI and NAME or CALLSIGN of own vessel – spoken three times. The text of the SAFETY MESSAGE. OUT

All Ships Safety call – voice

16	SECURITE, SECURITE, SECURITE. ALL STATIONS or called station – spoken three times. THIS IS – NAME of vessel three times. Text of MESSAGE – safety issue, position, etc. OUT

OTHER CALLS

Routine DSC calls

To make a routine call using DSC you need the MMSI of the station you are calling.

1 Select DIRECTORY if the MMSI is stored or MANUAL if not stored.
2 Enter the MMSI number.
3 Select a REPLY channel for the response (intership calling only).
4 Press ENTER to send the digital call.

Calling a marina – voice only

1 Note the relevant details of your vessel: LOA, beam, draft, etc, and nights you wish to stay.
2 Select the marina's working channel – generally CH80.
3 Switch to low power.
4 Listen to check the channel is clear by waiting 5 seconds.
5 Transmit your call:
   - MARINA NAME – once.
   - THIS IS – your vessel name twice.
   - OVER.
6 When you receive a reply, explain your reasons for calling and give your vessel details.
7 He will give you berthing instructions - write them down as he gives them.
8 Repeat the relevant information back.
9 Both stations sign OUT.

RADIO JARGON BUSTER

AIS Automatic Identification System. This system is used by shipping. It allows another vessel or coast station to use equipment that can interrogate the radio in order to learn the course, speed, type of vessel, cargo, etc. It will become available in the future to recreational vessels.

ALRS Vol. 1 Admiralty List of Radio Signals Volume 1

Authorised Operator The person with the VHF Short Range Certificate who also has an Authority to Operate.

Callsign Unique letter/number vessel identification number

CG66 Coastguard Yacht and Boat Safety Scheme form

Convention ships Cargo vessels over 300 Gross Registered Tons and passenger ships that carry 13 or more people.

COSPAS/SARSAT A satellite-aided search and rescue system designed to locate EPIRBS transmitting on 121.5 MHz and 406 MHz.

Distress A situation when a vessel, vehicle, aircraft or person is in grave and imminent danger and requests immediate assistance.

DSC Digital Selective Calling

DTI Department of Trade and Industry

Dual watch A facility that allows you to monitor CH16 and one other channel at the same time.

Duplex Radio working that uses two antennas for working on a two-frequency VHF channel.

EPIRB Electronic Position Indicating Radio Beacon

GHz Gigahertz

GMDSS Global Maritime Distress and Safety System

GMT Greenwich Mean Time

GPS Global Positioning System

HF High Frequency

HMCG Her Majesty's Coastguard

IMO International Maritime Organisation

INMARSAT International Mobile Satellite Organisation

ITU International Telecommunication Union

Mayday Distress signal. Origin French – *m'aidez* – help me.

MF Medium Frequency

MHz Megahertz.

MMSI 9-digit Maritime Mobile Service Identity

Navtex Maritime safety information broadcast received on 518 KHz and 490kHz as text

NBDP Narrow Band Direct-Printing, see Navtex

NMEA interface Marine industry standard method of connecting one piece of electronic equipment to another, eg GPS with autopilot.

Pan Pan Urgency signal. Origin French – *en panne* – in difficulty.

PTT Press to transmit switch

Public Correspondence Telephone communications

Radio Check Test call that asks 'What is the strength and clarity of my transmission?'

Radio horizon The distance the radio signal will travel before it reaches the horizon

RX Receive

SAR Search and Rescue

Securite Safety signal. Origin French – *sécurité* – safety

Semi-Duplex Radio working that uses one antenna to switch between two frequencies on one channel. One frequency for transmitting, the other for receiving.

Simplex Radio working that uses the same frequency for transmitting and receiving.

Squelch A radio control that suppresses background interference.

Traffic Radio messages

TX Transmitting

UHF Ultra High Frequency (300–3000MHz)

Urgency A situation that is not grave and imminent but serious

UTC Universal Co-ordinated Time. This is also known as GMT (Greenwich Mean Time). This is the basis for all calculations of time and it is the time shown on the display of a VHF-DSC radio. Times around the world are all related to UTC.

VHF Very High Frequency

Voluntary Fit Vessels that are not 'Convention Ships' (see Convention Ships).

VTS Vessel Traffic Services

Watt A measure of power output.

Useful Addresses

Royal Yachting Association
RYA House
Ensign Way, Hamble
Southampton
SO31 4YA
Tel: 0845 345 0400
Fax: 0845 345 0329
Web: www.rya.org.uk

Ofcom
Ofcom Contact Centre
Riverside House
2a Southwark Bridge Road
London
SE1 9HA
Tel: 0845 456 3000
or 020 7981 3040
Email: contact@ofcom.org.uk
Fax: 0845 456 3333
Web: www.ofcom.co.uk

Maritime Coastguard Agency
Spring Place
105 Commercial Road
Southampton
SO15 1EG
Tel: 0870 6006505
Email: infoline@mcga.gov.uk

RT Training
(SRC and LRC training provider)
286 Sea Front
Hayling Island
Hants
PO11 0AZ
United Kingdom
Phone/Fax: ++44 (0)2392 462122
Email: info@marineradio.co.uk
Web: www.marineradio.co.uk

Chichester Maritime Ltd
(RYA theory course provider)
PO Box 16
Hayling Island
PO11 0TS
Phone: 0207 0601126
or 0871 2180299
Email: sales@cmonline.co.uk
Web: www.cmonline.co.uk

Appendix 1
THE INTERNATIONAL MARITIME VHF BANDPLAN

Channel Number	Single Frequency	Dual Frequency	Ship Transmit	Coast Receive	Coast Transmit	Ship Receive	Distress Calling	Intership	Port ops Ship MVMT	Coast Radio Stn
1		✓	156.050	156.050	160.650	160.650			✓	✓
2		✓	156.100	156.100	160.700	160.700			✓	✓
3		✓	156.150	156.150	160.750	160.750			✓	✓
4		✓	156.200	156.200	160.800	160.800			✓	✓
5		✓	156.250	156.250	160.850	160.850			✓	✓
6	✓		156.300	156.300	156.300	156.300		✓		
7		✓	156.350	156.350	160.950	160.950			✓	✓
8	✓		156.400	156.400	156.400	156.400		✓		
9	✓		156.450	156.450	156.450	156.450		✓	✓	
10	✓		156.500	156.500	156.500	156.500		✓	✓	Oil pollution
11	✓		156.550	156.550	156.550	156.550		✓	✓	
12	✓		156.600	156.600	156.600	156.600		✓	✓	
13	✓		156.650	156.650	156.650	156.650		✓	✓	
14	✓		156.700	156.700	156.700	156.700			✓	
15	✓		156.750	156.750	156.750	156.750		✓	✓	Onboard coms
16	✓		156.800	156.800	156.800	156.800	✓		Distress, Safety &	Calling
17	✓		156.850	156.850	156.850	156.850			✓	Onboard coms
18		✓	156.900	156.900	161.500	161.500			✓	Onboard coms
19		✓	156.950	156.950	161.550	161.550			✓	
20		✓	157.000	157.000	161.600	161.600			✓	
21		✓	157.050	157.050	161.650	161.650			✓	
22		✓	157.100	157.100	161.700	161.700			✓	

Channel Number	Single Frequency	Dual Frequency	Ship Transmit	Coast Receive	Coast Transmit	Ship Receive	Distress Calling	Intership	Port ops Ship MVMT	Coast Radio Stn
22		✓	157.100	157.100	161.700	161.700			✓	
23		✓	157.150	157.150	161.750	162.750				
24		✓	157.200	157.200	161.800	161.800				
25		✓	157.250	157.250	161.850	161.850				
26		✓	157.300	157.300	161.900	161.900				
27		✓	157.350	157.350	161.900	161.900				
28		✓	157.400	157.400	162.000	162.000				
60		✓	156.025	156.025	160.625	160.625			✓	✓
61		✓	156.075	156.075	160.675	160.675			✓	✓
62		✓	156.125	156.125	160.725	160.725			✓	✓
63		✓	156.175	156.175	160.775	160.775			✓	✓
64		✓	156.225	156.225	160.825	160.825			✓	✓
65		✓	156.275	156.275	160.875	160.875			✓	✓
66		✓	156.325	156.325	160.925	160.925			✓	✓
67	✓		156.375	156.375	156.375	156.375		✓	HMCG	& SAR
68	✓		156.425	156.425	156.425	156.425			✓	✓
69	✓		156.475	156.475	156.475	156.475		✓		✓
70	✓		156.525	156.525	156.525	156.525	✓	Digital	Selective	Calling
71	✓		156.575	156.575	156.575	156.575			✓	
72	✓		156.625			156.625		✓		
73	✓		156.675	156.675	156.675	156.675		✓	HMCG	& SAR
74	✓		156.725	156.725	156.725	156.725		✓		✓
75	✓		156.775	156.775	156.775	156.775				Onboard comms. IW only
76	✓		156.825	156.775	156.775	156.775			✓	Onboard comms. IW only

Channel Number	Single Frequency	Dual Frequency	Ship Transmit	Coast Receive	Coast Transmit	Ship Receive	Distress Calling	Intership	Port ops Ship MVMT	Coast Radio Stn
77	✔		156.875			156.875		✔		
78		✔	156.925	156.925	161.525	161.525			✔	✔
79		✔	156.975	156.975	161.575	161.575			✔	✔
80		✔	157.025	157.025	161.625	161.625			✔	✔
81		✔	157.075	157.075	161.675	161.675			✔	✔
82		✔	157.125	157.125	161.725	162.725			✔	✔
83		✔	157.175	157.175	161.775	161.775				✔
84		✔	157.225	157.225	161.825	161.825			✔	
85		✔	157.275	157.275	161.875	161.875				✔
86		✔	157.325	157.325	161.925	161.925				✔
87			157.375			157.375			✔	
88			157.425			157.425			✔	
AIS 1	✔		161.975							
AIS 2	✔		162.025							

APPENDIX 2
THE SHORT RANGE CERTIFICATE SYLLABUS

1 General knowledge of VHF radiotelephone communications in the maritime mobile service.

1.1 Types of communication:
- distress, urgency and safety communications
- port operations service
- ship movement service
- intership communications
- onboard communications

1.2 Types of station: Ship station, coast station, etc

1.3 Elementary knowledge of radio frequencies and channels:
- VHF radiowave propagation
- range for voice communications and DSC transmissions
- simple, semi-duplex and duplex channels
- small craft safety channels
- intership communications
- port operations
- ship movement
- calling channels

1.4 Batteries

2 Detailed working knowledge of radio equipment

2.1 VHF radio functions and controls:
- channel selection and controls
- dual watch facilities and controls
- press to transmit switch
- high/low power output switch
- volume control
- squelch control
- dimmer

2.2 Portable VHF radios

2.3 VHF antennas

3 Purpose and use of Digital Selective Calling facilities
- **3.1** General principles and basic features of DSC
  - DSC messages
  - DSC attempt
  - call acknowledgement
  - call relay
- **3.2** Types of call:
  - distress call
  - all ships call
  - call to individual station
  - geographic area call
  - group call
- **3.3** Maritime Mobile Service Identity number system
- **3.4** Category and priority of calls:
  - distress
  - urgency
  - safety
  - ship's business
  - routine
- **3.5** VHF DSC facilities and usage
  - Channel 70
  - DSC data entry and display
  - DSC watchkeeping functions and controls

4 Operational procedures of the GMDSS
- **4.1** Distress communications via VHF DSC equipment:
  - DSC alert
  - definition of distress alert
  - transmission of a distress alert
  - transmission of a shore to ship distress alert relay
  - transmission of a distress alert by a station not itself in distress
  - receipt and acknowledgement of DSC distress alert
  - acknowledgement procedure by ship and shore stations
- **4.2** Urgency and safety communications via VHF DSC equipment:
  - meaning of urgency and safety communications
  - procedures for DSC urgency and safety calls
  - urgency communications
  - safety communications

APPENDIX 2

5 Protection of distress frequencies
- Avoiding harmful interference
- false alerts and procedure to follow when one is transmitted
- Channel 70
- transmissions during distress traffic
- prevention of unauthorised transmissions
- testing procedures
- VHF guardbands

6 Navtex

7 Alerting and locating signals

7.1 Emergency Position Indicating Radio Beacons (EPIRB) types
- registration and coding
- operation
- maintenance

7.2 Search and rescue transponder (SART)
- operation
- operating height
- effect of radar reflector
- range of SART transmitter

8 VHF radiotelephone procedures and regulations

8.1 Distress communications:
- correct use of Mayday signal
- distress call and message
- acknowledgement
- control of distress traffic
- correct use of the signal Mayday Relay
- transmission of a distress message by a station not itself in distress

8.2 Urgency communications:
- urgency signal
- correct use and meaning of Pan Pan
- urgency message
- obtaining urgent medical advice

8.3 Safety communications:
- safety signal
- correct use and meaning of Securite
- safety message

- special procedures for communication with appropriate national organisations on matters affecting safety

8.4 Reception of Maritime safety information

8.5 Use of Standard Marine Navigational vocabulary

8.6 Use of international phonetic alphabet

8.7 Awareness of international documentation and publications

8.8 Requirement for ship station licence

8.9 Regulations concerning the operation of the radio by the holder of an appropriate certificate of competence

8.10 Logbooks

8.11 Preservation of the secrecy of correspondence

8.12 Types of call and message that are prohibited

9 **Practical and theoretical knowledge of radiotelephone procedures**

9.1 Practical traffic routines:
- correct use of callsigns
- procedure for unanswered calls and garbled calls
- control of communication

9.2 Procedure for establishing communication on the following channels:
- intership
- small craft safety channel
- port operations
- ship movement

APPENDIX 2

INDEX

INDEX